SAM SZOR:

Toledo's Mr. Music

By Judy Harris Szor

The University of Toledo Press
Toledo, Ohio

2020

D1378086

The University of Toledo Press

www.utoledopress.com

Copyright 2020
By The University of Toledo Press

Manufactured in the United States of America

Sam Szor:
Toledo's Mr. Music

By Judy Harris Szor

Edited by Yarko Kuk
Project assistance from Erin Czerniak,
Madison Rane Vasko, and Steven Tozer Wipfli
Book design by Stephanie Delo

ISBN 978-1-7332664-3-7

Dedication

I dedicate this book to our grandchildren:
Patrick Hickey, Emily Hickey,
Caitlin Hickey Yanosko, Kelsey Hickey, Madison Hickey,
Lukas Kreutzer, Olivia Szor, and Francesca Szor.

TABLE OF CONTENTS

Acknowledgements

I am most appreciative to all those who gave me encouragement in the writing of this book. Most especially I am grateful to my late husband, Sam, who kept such complete records that this job was a little less daunting than it otherwise would have been.

Thank you to Tom Szor, who was essential in many ways, from filling in family history information, to calling on his amazing memory of events, to discussions that helped me sort out how and what I wanted to communicate about Sam, as well as locating photos. He was also one of the readers of the manuscript who offered some editing and comments.

Byron West was especially helpful with information from Sam's younger years, as were Tom Bollin and John Beddoes with information from his Woodward High School and University of Toledo years.

Tom Bollin, Beth White, Patti Beach, and Joanna Russ contributed as readers of the manuscript who made comments and helped with editing. I am so very appreciative of their time and efforts as their contributions made this a better book.

Thank you to my niece, Allyson Harris Robinson, who photographed all of Sam's awards and recognitions, and to The University of Toledo Press and Yarko Kuk for the expert editing and publishing of this book.

And finally, thank you to all of these people, in addition to those mentioned above, who were so gracious in taking their time to make contributions to this book: Ruth Brown Shaw, Robert Bell, Steve Janick, Bud Kerwin, Karen Benson Werner, Vivian Bowling Blevins, Marie Reuter Troxell, Phillip Kaufman, Fred Cieslewski, Beth Henderson, Dick Martin, Tom Treece, Dan Duvendack, Diane Lamberton Spahr, Aida Garcia Cardenas, Mike Spahr, Judy Hauman Dye, Keith McWatters, Clark Barnes, Joe Meyers, Lorraine Ray, Shannon Ford, Kim Bryden

1

Loch, Martha Reikow, Roger Samonek, John Bartko, Beth Swartz O'Shea, Mark Danisovszky, and Ron Wade. It is your stories that help make the book come alive.

Introduction

My first motivation for writing this book was to present it as a gift to Sam's grandchildren so they, in adulthood, might have a greater understanding and appreciation of who their grandfather was. I felt it was especially important for the two youngest who, due to distance, were not able to see him often and were only ages three and seven when he died. As I began thinking about the book, what to include and how to organize it, I presented the idea to some friends and colleagues. Their responses were enthusiastic and supportive and all said it would be a book they would definitely want to read.

As I reached out to former students and colleagues of Sam's to begin gathering information, I continued to receive encouraging comments and requests to please let them know when the book is complete. A couple of people asked if I was prepared to write a 2,000-page book as surely it would take that many pages to try to capture Sam and all he accomplished. The task was indeed daunting. I knew I could not write 2,000 pages, but I was committed to giving it my best effort.

So, encouraged by those with whom I spoke, my idea morphed from a casual booklet intended primarily for the family, to a substantial book to be read by anyone interested.

Sam was known as "Toledo's Mr. Music." We don't know for sure how or when he was awarded that moniker, perhaps it was bestowed upon him or maybe it was something that evolved over time because Sam was everywhere, or at least it seemed so. Everywhere there was music, there was Sam. If someone needed music for an occasion, one could always call on Sam and be confident that whatever it was, it would be done and done exceptionally well.

The book is a biography of his professional life—musician, teacher, coach, friend—accounting his many accomplishments. But more than that, it chronicles the profound impact his burst of talent had on Toledo and surrounding communities for six decades.

Judy Harris Szor

Chapter 1
The Early Years

Sam Szor's parents, Samuel Szor and Mary Bacso, were both born in the United States—Samuel in 1903 in Toledo, and Mary in 1907 in Brownstown, Pennsylvania. The children of Hungarian immigrants, both were taken back to Hungary by their parents, Mary as an infant, and Samuel during grade school, after his father was killed in a fire at Interlake Iron on Front Street, where he worked. Though a difficult journey, it was not uncommon for families to go back and forth between the "old country" and the United States. Because they had been born in the U.S., Samuel and Mary were American citizens and able to return to the U.S. of their own accord. When she was about 16-years-old, Mary traveled alone from Goncruszka, Hungary to Toledo, where she lived with her cousins, the Joseph Vargo family. When he was 22, Samuel, along with his mother, sister, and half-brother, moved from Abauj Megye, Hungary back to Toledo. Both families settled in the Birmingham ethnic neighborhood on Toledo's east side. Mary worked as a live-in nanny and domestic until she was married, and Samuel took a job at Interlake Iron where his father had died years before.

Samuel and Mary met at their neighborhood church and married on May 5, 1928. Once they were married, Mary continued part-time work as a domestic, even after her children were born. She also worked at Willys-Overland, sewing canvas for the tops of Jeeps that were being built for World War II.

Sam, about 6-years-old, on a pony in the Birmingham neighborhood.

Their first child, Samuel Paul Szor (Sam) was born May 22, 1930 in the Szor family home at 2354 Bakewell Street, in the Birmingham neighborhood. In 1936, the family moved to a home three blocks away at 2431 Caledonia Street, which would be the Szor family home for more than four decades. Sam and his younger sisters—Elizabeth, born in 1936, and twin sisters Joyce and Joann, born in 1941—would grow up in and around one of Toledo's vibrant ethnic neighborhoods.

Birmingham was a neighborhood of immigrant families. At the time, Hungarians made up most of the residents, but there were also Slovaks, Czechs, Italians, and Bulgarians. It was a closely knit, safe, and immaculately cared for neighborhood. Sam's family owned an additional lot that they used for a garden. As soon as he was old enough, Sam would help spade and plant the garden every spring. The family garden always included Italian parsley and kohlrabi for Hungarian chicken soup, along with many other vegetables. The root vegetables were kept buried under the back porch, which served as a makeshift "root cellar" and supplied the family for much of the winter.

Sam often recalled fond memories of the old neighborhood, from the Italians who played bocce ball in their yards on Sunday afternoons, to the Czechs who practiced gymnastics and held exhibitions at Sokol Hall at the corner of Valentine and Moravan Streets. He had fond memories of taking his sister Elizabeth (Liz) on outings when she was old enough, especially on Sundays when they would go to the Tivoli Theater, at 2225 Consaul, or across the river to downtown Toledo, to see a movie. The family never owned a car, so they went everywhere on foot or by bus.

He would also recount the story of the birth of his twin sisters with a smile on his face. They were born at home—as both Sam and Liz had been—the day after his mother had been wallpapering the ceiling of the dining room. When the doctor arrived, young Sam was sent out of the house. When he returned home, the doctor was on the porch smoking a cigarette and said, "you have a baby sister." Sam promptly set out to alert everyone in the neighborhood of the arrival of his new baby sister. When he returned home, the doctor was again on the porch smoking another cigarette. Sam asked if everything was okay, and the doctor replied, "you have another baby sister." What a surprise! So, Sam was off again, updating all the neighbors with the joyous news of new twin girls at the Szor house.

A favorite childhood memory Sam often shared was about his birthday party. He had gone to many but had never had a birthday party of his own. So, in 1938, when his birthday happened to fall on a Sunday, Sam took it upon himself to invite his entire Sunday school class to his house for a birthday party that afternoon, unbeknownst to his mother. His mother, fondly known to all as "Grandma Szor," was a wonderful cook and baker and was able to come up with something to serve to the party goers, despite being caught totally off guard.

Like other ethnic neighborhoods in Toledo, Birmingham was self-contained, with its own churches, doctors, pharmacies, grocery and dry goods stores, bakeries, banks, taverns, restaurants, attorneys, and more. There was little need to venture outside the community, consequently Sam didn't speak English until he started public school. He said the only English words he knew before going to school were "airplane" and "ice cream."

Every Sunday morning, as Sam walked to church, he would smell the Hungarian chicken soup cooking in the kitchens of nearly every house along the way. On his way home, he would deliver copies of the church's Sunday bulletin, *Kislap*, to any neighbors who were unable to attend church that day. The church was central in the lives of the Szor family when Sam was growing up. Most activities revolved around the church, which for them was the Hungarian Reformed Church on Bakewell Street in Birmingham. At the time, all services and activities at the church were conducted in Hungarian. In addition to the religious services, there were dances—where the boys had to learn to dance the csárdás with their mothers, much to the dismay of the boys—dinners, festivals, youth groups, choirs, and more at the church. Hungarian church music is sung with gusto, and music is an important part of both the service and the culture Sam started singing in the adult choir at church as a youth and continued to do so until he left home for college. These early musical experiences in the church and the community nurtured his interest in music.

Sam's eighth-grade confirmation was a significant event. The final step of his confirmation included addressing the entire congregation and answering questions, in Hungarian of course. In those years, in the eyes of the church, confirmation meant you had become a man, and Sam took this new level of responsibility very seriously. He

Sam's confirmation picture.

continued to be very involved in the church throughout his high school years and, for a time, considered entering the ministry.

In addition to his immediate family, Birmingham was home to a number of Sam's relatives, including his father's sister and her husband, Mary Elizabeth and John Kaduk, who lived across the street with their children Elizabeth, Lola, John, Jr., and Ethel. Another cousin, Lola Vargo, was older than Sam and someone he looked up to. She played saxophone in the Waite High School band. Their shared love of music was a bond for Sam and Lola. Other family musicians included Sam's father, who played the concertina, and his father's half-brother, Benjamin, (Uncle Beni) who was pretty good on the violin.

Sam and his cousin, John Kaduk, were about the same age and were good friends. John was, by all accounts, a big, good-looking athletic boy. Sam, on the other hand, was physically average in stature and had vision only in his left eye. The cause of his loss of vision was never clear; the

A 10-year-old Sam with his saxophone. Sam started playing both saxophone and clarinet in the fourth grade.

debate was between a congenital cataract or injury to his right eye during birth. He did eventually have his eye removed at the recommendation of an ophthalmologist when he was in his thirties and had a prosthesis thereafter. At any rate, without depth perception, although he played some sports, they were not his forté. In music, however, he had no handicap.

Sam attended Birmingham Elementary School in east Toledo. It was there he began to learn English, and, when he was in the fourth grade, started music lessons at his request. He began on saxophone and clarinet, having private lessons from a teacher who came to the house. He didn't talk much about his grade school years, but he stuck with the music lessons, so he must have liked them. One of Sam's former students, John Beddoes, said his great aunt was one of Sam's teachers at Birmingham school and remembered "Sammy" fondly as a smart, funny, and enthusiastic boy. Beddoes described his aunt as a very dignified and reserved woman, but said when she talked about Sam, it was clear to him that even as an eight-year-old, Sam already had a high "lovability factor." As time went on, she was always interested in hearing about what Sam was doing.

Sam met Byron (By) West in a youth orchestra at Garfield Elementary School when By was in sixth grade and Sam was in eighth. Toledo Public School music teacher Mrs. Knold selected talented students from many schools for the orchestra. By the time Sam was in junior high, he was already playing gigs with local Slovak and Czek bands. Also around this time—the early 1940s—music theory classes were taught at the Toledo Museum of Art on Saturday mornings by Beverly Barksdale, who went on to become manager of the Cleveland Symphony Orchestra. In addition to playing in the youth orchestra, Sam and By would meet every Saturday morning to take the music theory classes at the museum. The pair would meet up at Adams and Superior streets in downtown Toledo, where they would get the long belt street car down Monroe Street to the

Toledo Museum of Art. After class, they would walk downtown to get a sandwich at the Toddle House or a similar eatery. The pair went on to attend Waite High School where they continued to build their knowledge and skills in music. Rooted in music, Sam and By's friendship lasted a lifetime.

Those who knew Sam as a child and young man described him as being very quiet. It may have been because he was self-conscious about the appearance of his bad eye. However, when he was in high school, Sam made a conscious decision to try to become more outgoing and get more out of life. He blossomed into an outgoing, fun, and charismatic person, becoming quite popular in high school and beyond.

Cecile Vashaw

At Waite High School Sam took college prep courses and became very involved in the school's music programs, both instrumental and vocal. He joined the band, which was under the direction of New York University-educated Cecile Vashaw. Vashaw was a very progressive woman who would become a major influence in Sam's life. He initially played saxophone in marching band until earning the leadership role of drum major his senior year. As drum major, Sam learned to twirl the baton by watching other twirlers and by going to clinics, eventually teaching baton classes himself and judging competitions. With his limited depth perception, it's always been somewhat of a mystery how he managed to twirl and toss the baton so well, but somehow Sam figured it out. In concert band, when the school purchased a bassoon, Vashaw assigned it to Sam. She obviously saw potential in him, as in addition to being drum major and playing the bassoon, she had Sam oversee her seventh period girls chorus class when she had other things she needed to do. He loved this role and the

Sam, center, was Band Major his senior year at Waite High School.

teasing from all the girls.

His fellow students took note of his leadership abilities. One year he was the campaign manager for a girl who was running for student council president. At the last minute, when it became clear that she was not going to win, one of the teachers suggested running Sam as a write-in candidate, unbeknownst to him. Some of his friends quickly formed the "Bull Moose Party" and were at all the school doors the next morning promoting Sam as a write-in candidate. Amazingly, he won the election, but was convinced by Vashaw that he had to resign because he could not fulfill his band and class responsibilities while serving as student council president.

Waite's marching band had a rare opportunity in 1947. The school's football team was undefeated that season, as was the football team for Austin High School in El Paso, Texas. Somehow a "playoff" game was arranged to determine which team was the "national champion" in high school football. The Waite band traveled by train to El Paso to march at the game. It was quite an experience for this group of high school students, most of whom had hardly been out of Toledo before. With winds gusting up to 30 mph and a big cheering section made up of soldiers from nearby Fort Bliss, Waite beat Austin 20-12. The following year the Austin football team came to Toledo for a re-match, and Waite won again, this time 20-13.

Sam's other musical endeavors while in high school included singing in the high school choir (of which he was president) and a barbershop quartet he helped form. The barbershop quartet used to enter competitions on WSPD radio but always lost out to Teresa Brewer, who lived across the back alley from Sam. She frequently sang "Old Man Mose Done Kicked the Bucket, Buck-, Buck-, Bucket" and danced to it, even when they were competing on the radio.

In 1944, Sam, along with other members of the Waite High School band, established their own dance band called the Paul Mabie Band. They had thirteen pieces in the band in which Sam and his friend By both played saxophone. Teresa Brewer also sang with the band on occasion.

The Paul Mabie band. Sam is in the front row, center. His friend, By West, is to Sam's right.

The Toledo Young People's Orchestra, the precursor to the Toledo Youth Orchestra. Sam is in back row (indicated with white arrow). His friend By West is a row in front of Sam, just to the left of Sam.

She went on to a successful singing career—one of her best known tunes being "Music! Music! Music! (Put Another Nickel In)." The band had no help from any teacher or adult. They found the charts they wanted, rehearsed on their own, and booked their own gigs. They played for high school proms in and around Toledo and as far south as Kenton, Ohio, as well as dances at Bowling Green State University, Toledo University, Catawba Island, and fraternity and sorority houses in Ann Arbor. They even made a 78 rpm record in 1948. The band disbanded in 1950 as the members moved on to new stages in their lives.

Sam and By embarked on another adventure together in 1948 when they joined the Toledo Young People's Symphony Orchestra. It was another student-organized group. According to an article in the February 2, 1948 edition of *The Toledo Blade*, the group began with a handful of students from DeVilbiss High School who gathered each week in a private home to go through the music of Mozart, Haydn, Bach, and other composers, "just for fun." Word spread and the group grew to 30 students, ranging from 11- to 20-years-old, from the Toledo area who were really interested music. A senior from DeVilbiss, Joseph Henry, was the group's conductor. Sam played the bassoon which gave him more experience with the instrument and an introduction to orchestral classical music. They performed symphonic works at Macomber High School and used a piggy bank to collect coins to pay for printing of programs for their concerts. This group was the forerunner of the present-day Toledo Youth Orchestra, according to Robert Bell, former President and CEO of the Toledo Symphony Orchestra.

During his senior year at Waite, Vashaw asked Sam what he planned to do after high school. Sam had never considered a career in music.

Music was not considered a "real" job by his parents, so, being good in math and science, Sam said he would probably go to Toledo University or Bowling Green State University to study engineering. Vashaw is reported to have told him: "get your instruments, I'm taking you up to play for Dr. [William] Revelli at University of Michigan." Sam didn't know anything about the University of Michigan or who Revelli was, but he got his horns and away

Sam's senior picture.

they went to the appointment Vashaw had arranged. After he auditioned on saxophone, clarinet, and bassoon, Revelli said he would like to have Sam join the school's band. Sam asked about scholarship money, but it was already gone. Revelli, however, said he could offer him a position on the library staff for the band that would pay fairly well. Upon their return to Toledo, Vashaw announced to Sam's parents that he would be attending the University of Michigan in the fall and majoring in music. And so it was.

Chapter 2
The University of Michigan

In the fall of 1948 Sam boarded a bus and headed to Ann Arbor to begin his studies at the University of Michigan (U of M). This marked a pair of milestones for Sam. It was the first time he was living outside of his beloved Birmingham neighborhood, and would also be the first time in his life he would be speaking English all day. The U of M experience had a profound impact on his life.

He initially lived in the East Quad dormitory, where he met fellow students from across the country and some from other parts of the world. As an upper classman, he joined Phi Gamma Delta fraternity. The Phi Gams wanted to do better in the annual songfest competition, so Sam took the reins. They had never placed in the top ten in the competition before, but the year with Sam at the helm, they came in second. One of his tenors was fraternity brother Bob McGrath, who would later become nationally-known as Bob Johnson on Sesame Street, a role he played for more than 40 years. With Toledo a mere 55 miles down the road from Ann Arbor, Sam returned to his beloved Birmingham neighborhood for the holidays, often bringing along friends who lived too far away to go to their own home, and who quickly learned to appreciate "Grandma Szor's" Hungarian cooking and pastries.

Most of Sam's time at U of M was not spent in his dorm, but in the school of music. At the time the school was housed in Harris Hall, a relatively small building at 617 E. Huron St. Sam recalled the bathroom was in the basement, and the stalls were so small that if you sat down on the commode your knees would open the door. He said Harris Hall proved one doesn't need glamorous surroundings to be able to learn, because there was a "million-dollar education" going on in that building every day. He said his bassoon teacher, Hugh Cooper, was one of the best teachers he ever had. According to Sam, Cooper was a nice man, but he didn't like to waste time. Occasionally, when Sam had not gotten in enough practice between lessons, Cooper could tell right away. He would just stop the lesson and say, "let's go get coffee." There was no apologizing or excuse making, just off they would go, point well made, with more practicing to come the next week.

Sam quickly rose to the top of the library staff for the band, becoming head librarian, perhaps as early as his sophomore year, which was remarkable. It was a major responsibility that continued through his senior year. Because of it, he spent a lot of time with Revelli, not just working with him, but driving him to and from the airport and working as a personal assistant. Sam even got to know Revelli's family. Revelli was a world-renowned band director and had a full schedule of guest conducting and clinics. It was Revelli's ability to evoke a band sound reminiscent of an orchestra that impressed Sam so very much. Sam used to tell the story of how, upon hearing the U of M band for the first time, it brought tears to his eyes because it was so beautiful. "If you closed your eyes and just listened, you would have thought it was a symphony orchestra," Sam recalled. "Revelli had a real gift." The February 10, 2010 edition of *Michigan Today* included an article, "Ode to Joy," by James Tobin. In it, Revelli is described as a talented, imposing figure:

> Other band directors said their students played better for Revelli, as a guest conductor, than for themselves. U-M leaders deferred to him. Don Canham, a legendary figure in his own right as athletic director from 1968 to 1988, once said: "I wouldn't have dared tell Revelli what to do." The commander-

conductor of the U.S. Air Force Band declared that "football has its Vince Lombardi, Symphony Orchestra has its Toscanini, the film industry its John Wayne. The bigger than life figure in the history of the American Band movement is clearly Dr. William D. Revelli."

While he appreciated his ability, Sam, however, was not particularly impressed with what he perceived as Revelli's sometimes unfair treatment of students. He ended up confronting Revelli about it, and they were able to continue to work together. Upon Sam's graduation, Revelli told him, "We never got along—or was it, we never did see eye to eye—but we got a lot done." Years later, Sam invited his former professor to guest conduct at Music Under the Stars a couple of times. On one occasion, as he introduced Revelli to the band, Sam commented, "I love him because he is so magical with sound." When Revelli stepped down from the podium, he said to Sam, "I love you too," confirming their mutual respect for one and other.

The U of M marching band in those years was all men, as marching was considered to be too strenuous for women. Sam played saxophone in the marching band, but when Revelli found out he could twirl the baton he wanted him to audition to be a twirler, to be one of the "men up front." Sam was reluctant, but Revelli insisted.

According to Sam, a national champion twirler was auditioning at the same time. Sam threw a horizontal toss and turned to watch the twirler. When Sam turned back, the wind had caught his baton and it came down on his face with the heavy leaded end hitting him squarely on nose. The audition ended with a trip to the emergency room to get his nose put back in place. Even that mishap did not change Revelli's mind, so Sam became a Michigan twirler for his junior and senior years.

Sam often said the twirlers covered more yards than the running backs on the football team. Twirlers would run out through the tunnel, onto and around the field, then up through the center of the band. The "men up front" consisted of two twirlers and the drum major. Every home game they were introduced to the crowd by name and hometown.

There were a couple of very memorable band events that Sam used to talk about. One was marching in what is known as the "Snow Bowl." Michigan faced off against Ohio State on Nov. 25, 1950, in Ohio Stadium, battling for the Big Ten conference football championship. The weather was miserable, with snow coming down at a rate of two

Sam as a twirler at the University of Michigan.

inches an hour, temperatures in the teens, and winds gusting over 25 mph. Field markings and even the goal posts were nearly impossible to see. While the teams played at one end of the field, snowplows worked feverishly trying to clear the opposite end. Michigan won 9-3 without ever making a first down.

After the game, the Ohio State Patrol was telling people to stay put, but Revelli insisted the band was going back to Ann Arbor that day. The buses only got as far as Delaware, Ohio, according to Sam's friend By West, and that was only after the guys had already been out of the buses several times to push them out of the snow. The band slept on the buses that night on a street in Delaware. It was slow going the next day, but they pushed on. When they finally got to Toledo, Revelli asked Sam where they could stop to eat. Sam wasn't sure what would be open—the snow was still bad and few people were out—but he thought Rudy's Hotdog would be worth a try. The busses, loaded with more than 100 hungry college men, made it to Sylvania Avenue, where both Rudy's and another hot dog place were open. The eateries were thrilled to see the buses pull up. They had to hustle, but got everyone fed, and forever after Sam got free hot dogs when he went to Rudy's on Sylvania Avenue.

In 1951, when the Wolverines faced the California Golden Bears in the Rose Bow, the U of M band made the trip to California on a fifteen-car private train, all paid for by Buick. Sam recalled the great fun the band had when the percussion section started playing rhythms in the diner car on the train—using utensils, glasses, plates, tables and anything else they could find—the car really rocked, he said.

They stopped along the way to march in parades in Wichita, Phoenix, and Albuquerque, and at every stop, they played the Buick theme song. It was in Albuquerque that the parade route had Christmas decorations strung across the street, so Revelli said no baton tosses. At the very end of the parade though, Sam couldn't resist letting his baton fly. It hit some of the decorations strung over the street which broke and rained down on Revelli, who was following the twirlers and was less than happy. It was something that still made Sam laugh many years later.

After marching in the Tournament of Roses Parade and performing during halftime of the Rose Bowl (Michigan defeated the California Golden Bears 14-6) they were off to San Francisco where they marched at halftime of the San Francisco 49ers football game the next day. They stopped at the Grand Canyon on their return journey.

Having played in dance bands for years before heading to Ann Arbor, Sam wanted to continue to do so. He enjoyed it and it was a way to make some money, even though that type of music was not condoned by the U of M School of Music at the time. He said they probably would have gotten in trouble if they had been found out, but he, as well as his friend By, continued to play with a band or two while at Michigan. Sometimes they would sneak off to Ypsilanti to play jazz in a club with Blind Bess. Sam used to tell the story of how they once accepted a Saturday night gig in Houghton, Michigan, in the upper peninsula. They didn't realize it was over 500 miles and a ferry ride to get there. It was like taking a one-night gig in New York City.

Each summer during his undergraduate years, Sam worked full-time at the Libbey-Owens-Ford (L-O-F) sheet glass factory in Rossford and played in local dance bands and clubs. He told the story of going to the plant to start work and being refused a job because he only had one eye. His uncle was president of the union at L-O-F at the time, and happened to stop at Sam's home. He asked why Sam was at home and not at work, and Sam told him what had happened. His uncle said, "I'll take care of it. Go back to work." There was never another question and Sam worked at the factory each summer, which gave him good income to help pay for school.

Even though he was playing in local dance bands and clubs, Sam still wanted to do more music in the summer. In 1950 he started the East Toledo Youth Chorus. The group rehearsed Wednesday and Friday

The East Toledo Youth Chorus Sam founded and conducted. Sam is in the front row, on the left.

nights at St. Mark's Lutheran Church on Woodville Road. They sang at various churches throughout the summer. Each year the chorus grew in size, and by 1952 it had 50 members ranging in age from 16- to 22-years-old. They changed their name to the Toledo Youth Chorus, as they had members from every high school in Toledo, Waterville, and Ottawa Hills, as well as eleven universities. The 1952 chorus even had a business manager who handled bookings and an entertainment chairman who arranged picnics and outings. They sang at a church every Sunday and were even special guests at Music Under the Stars (MUTS). Started in 1946, MUTS was as a series of Sunday evening concerts in various parks around the city. In 1950 MUTS was moved to the Toledo Zoo Amphitheater, where it enjoyed great success for more than 60 years.

Sam graduated with a Bachelor of Music Education in June of 1952. After graduating, he married Marjorie McLean whom he met at U of M. Their union produced four children: Thomas born in 1954, Terry born in 1956, Megan born in 1959, and Martha born in 1963. Grandchildren include Patrick, Emily, Caitlin, Kelsey, and Madison, born to Megan and her husband, Paul Hickey; Lukas Samuel Kreutzer son of Martha; and Olivia and Francesca, daughters of Terry. Sam and Marjorie divorced in 1973.

Sam married Judy Harris in 1975, with whom he spent the rest of his life and who became his "right hand 'man.'" In addition to music, the pair shared a love of gardening, cooking, traveling and entertaining. Their trips to New York City allowed Sam to stay current with Broadway shows, information he used for concert programming. Sam and Judy also enjoyed trips to Europe. In 1987 they took Sam's mother to Hungary for her 80th birthday so she could visit her brothers and sisters. On another trip, Sam and Judy spent ten days in London, during which they saw fourteen musicals and ballet performances. Costa Rica was their most frequently visited place. Sam was equally at home cooking on the grill and slow cooking in the oven, and their gardens contained lots of Italian parsley and kohlrabi along with many other vegetables, just like his parents' garden.

Upon graduating from the University of Michigan in 1952, despite a number of good job offers out of state, Sam was convinced by his former high school band teacher, Cecile Vashaw, and others, that he owed it to Toledo to come back to his hometown to share his talents, which is exactly what he did.

Chapter 3
Woodward High School

Sam's first job out of college was band director at Woodward High School in Lagrinka, which at the time was a predominantly Polish neighborhood in north Toledo. Sam often told the story of his first day of teaching. He was very nervous, and when he started to call the roll for band class he failed miserably in his pronunciation of students' names. He struggled so much that he was forced to spell many of them. The final straw was the name Pryzbysz (pronounced Pshibish). "There wasn't a vowel in there," he would say with a laugh. It didn't take long for him to catch on though, and soon he was learning and speaking whole phrases in Polish, endearing himself to the community.

I wasn't a student, but Sam brought the band to practice behind the old Point Place Junior High. My family lived next to the school and Sam walked over one day and I then learned that my father knew Sam, and then Sam asked about my grandfather. Gramps had a gypsy band that had played in the Birmingham neighborhood. Sam and dad would sit in our back yard during band breaks and talk about old times. What a great man Sam was.

John Bartko

When he started in the fall of 1952, Sam's top priority was getting the marching band ready for football games. He was never one to put less than his best foot forward, so he had a lot of work to do. Accounts vary, but when Sam took over the program, there were between fifteen and 40 students in the band. He took whoever had signed up for band, of course, but then set about recruiting more students. Sam talked with other teachers and reviewed the individual records of students in the school. When he found a student who was successful in their studies, he would approach them about joining the band, and boy, was he a good salesman. His former students said he had such positive energy and enthusiasm that it was difficult, if not impossible, to say no. He built the band to 60, then 80, and finally nearly 100 musicians by his third year, along with eight majorettes, two twirlers, and one drum major. The majorettes were also required to play an instrument.

> *I did not play in the band, but everybody in the school knew Sam because he always had such a big smile and so much energy and enthusiasm for what he was doing. I was amazed at how Sam quickly turned a very average band into a spectacular band which was a source of pride for everyone in the school.*
>
> *Fred Cieslewski*
> *Woodward High School, Class of 1956*

Sam was a firm believer that opportunities for students to perform served as motivation for them to learn, gave them satisfaction in goal accomplishment, and would build camaraderie among the group. The band performed at all football games, a variety of other athletic events,

The Woodward High School concert band, around 1955.

as well as the usual school concerts several times a year. In addition, they were frequently seen in parades as, the dedication of new buildings and signs, the opening of the Community Chest Drive, and other significant events around town. Years later, when driving down Interstate 75 from Michigan, Sam would often comment that the Woodward band helped dedicate the "Welcome to Ohio" sign at the border, just as they did the Robert Craig Memorial Bridge in 1957.

Robert Bell, who was a freshman when Sam began at Woodward, went on to make a career with the Toledo Symphony Orchestra in several capacities, including President and CEO for many years. On the occasion of Bell's induction into the Woodward Hall of Fame he wrote, "Sam was the single most powerful influence on my life during a particularly impressionable time of growing up. He helped nurture the passion for musical discovery and the confidence in my ability that was to be so essential to my future."

Sam was the first significant male figure in my life, and I learned so much from him. As a freshman I had started in orchestra, then Sam invited me to join the band. I didn't have much self-confidence, but Sam saw some potential in me that I didn't know was there. He was responsible for me feeling better about myself.

Eventually I became almost like a personal assistant to Sam and spent a lot of time with him, hauling equipment and setting up for concerts, sometimes driving him up to Ann Arbor when he was working on his Masters' Degree so he could study during the trip. That's when I began to develop an interest in classical music.

From the time I spent with Sam I learned work ethic and the importance of things like having every chair and stand in the right place. There was a side of Sam that was so compelling—his enthusiasm, energy and his determination to get things done, in spite of obstacles and limited resources. He was a Jack of all Trades who wore many hats. I learned from all of that and it has helped me in all my work in music over the years. I probably would not have had any career in music if not for Sam.

Robert Bell
Woodward High School, Class of 1956

The Woodward High School band's halftime shows were spectacular. Sam's creative juices really flowed in the ideas and the planning, and as the students became more engaged, he involved them in the creative responsibilities as well. The halftime shows often included costumes for the majorettes, and sometimes for the whole band. One student, Dina Grevis Costa, designed many of the costumes and sewed some of them

Members of the marching band in costume for the Russian Show.

too. Often the majorettes or their mothers would sew the costumes after the designs were completed. The costumes were exceptional, and certainly did not appear to be home made. The half-time shows were usually performed twice, once at home and once at an away game. Some of the halftime shows included: *Loch Lomond*, *Mambo Italiano*, *My Fair Lady*, and *The King and I* (1956); Japanese Show, *West Side Story* (the majorettes did interpretive ballet), Russian Show (the whole band was in costume), and *Gigi* (1959); Music of Stephen Foster (majorettes all learned to play banjo), *Peter Pan*, *Can-Can*, and *Flower Drum Song* (1961); and Swingin' Dancers, Drum Show, Israeli Show, *Camelot*, and *Wizard of Oz* (1962).

I have so very many fond memories of Mr. Szor. He was one of a kind! In August 1962 at Point Place Junior High field—band camp it's called now—I'm at my first one and only had five months playing my flute. It's just before my junior year and I can barely play a scale let alone keep up with the great musicians we had. The song was "Big D" and it was way too fast for this beginner player. Mr. Szor was running up and down the field egging us on. Suddenly I hear him over his megaphone, "someone's out of step—I'm not saying her name, but her initials are RUTH BROWN." I'm mortified but hang in there and eventually got pretty good on the instrument.

The majorettes who learned how to play the banjo.

He also regularly grabbed a baton inadvertently dropped by a majorette or twirler and put on a show throwing it twenty feet into the air and catching it. There are just way too many stories to relate, but band and Mr. Szor are burned into my brain. When I am a really old lady in my rocking chair I will remember with great joy those days and people.

Ruth Brown Shaw
Woodward High School, Class of 1964

As Woodward High School band director, Sam was responsible for the marching band, concert band, and pep band. He also added a jazz band. Sam also went to the grade schools and junior high a couple of times a week to teach beginning music classes and start students on instruments. This served as a recruitment opportunity, paying off in the years to follow.

My first exposure to Sam was in 1956 when he came to Point Place Junior High (PPJH) to teach a one-hour band class twice a week. It could be a tough neighborhood for a small boy with a clarinet. Back then bullying was an unfettered art form and often directed at boys who either carried books or a musical instrument. There were times when I had to deal with bullies who wanted to play keep-away with my horn. During the three years I spent a PPJH, I collected a couple of broken noses. Despite the guff, I soon discovered there was an offset in the form of Samuel P. Szor. He shared his joy for music with us and thoroughly convinced us that we were doing something cool. Most of us became "true believers" and moved to Woodward High School, joining the marching band, orchestra, or choir.

Sam's tenure at Woodward was a huge success that was largely personality driven. His success with his students, parents, administration, and fellow teachers was the result of his ability to relate to individuals and make them feel like they mattered. He always remembered names and could recall names and details of former students half a century down the road. He always took the time to know every person in his band and as much about them as possible.

Sam had a group of loyal band members who would go the extra mile for him. It was an "inner-circle" that usually numbered at least a dozen, but on occasion expanded to include literally everyone and his or her brother. I frequently ran errands for Sam, because I could drive and could also be trusted not to screw up. For example, Sam had me drive his new '61 Pontiac Tempest over to his home on Drummond Road to collect his pay check, which he'd forgotten to deposit. When I got there and looked in his desk, I found three paychecks. Two from the Board of Education and one from the American Federation of Musicians. I brought him all three checks because I figured that if I left them, he'd probably neglect whatever I left behind. [He was] a man who had so many irons in the fire, he often overlooked his own needs.

John Beddoes
Woodward High School, Class of 1962

Sam was always looking for ways to challenge and help students grow and to improve their performances. To that end, he asked Bud Kerwin, who graduated from Woodward in 1954 and had started a dance studio in the area, to teach ballet to the majorettes starting in the mid-1950s. Kerwin said it was a hard sell at first; the majorettes were resistant. But Sam talked with their twirling teacher who got on board and helped turn it around. The dance training created a much more professional and sophisticated appearance of the majorettes and enhanced the performance of the whole band; parents and faculty were very impressed with the talent of the students and what they could do. The success was contagious and the dance program grew. In addition to his band responsibilities, Woodward had a tradition of an annual Extravaganza—an all-school musical production—that Sam continued.

Initially, Kerwin went to Woodward after school to work with the majorettes, but then Sam had ideas for the Extravaganzas. Sam started recruiting more students to take dance classes in preparation for the Extravaganzas. Eventually the students started going to Kerwin's studio for classes, both boys and girls. When asked how they recruited the boys, Kerwin said, "I don't know because Sam said, 'don't worry, they'll be there,' and they always were."

Steve Janick, Woodward High School class of 1963, got involved when he was a freshman. He said Sam made an announcement asking all freshman boys in good academic standing to report to a specific classroom after school. No reason was given. Janick said about 35 to 40 boys came. Sam explained the tradition of the Extravaganzas and with his personality, enthusiasm, and energy, was able to convince several, including Janick, to sign up. Janick ended up dancing all through high school, the University of Michigan, and for some years after. He became part of Kerwin's company, as Kerwin agreed to teach these students from Woodward free of charge on the understanding that they would dance as part of his company. The company included students from other schools and is how Janick met the girl who later became his wife.

As more students came to classes, Kerwin was able to teach partnering and lifting, allowing the company to expand its repertoire. This was beneficial to the students, to Woodward High School, and to Kerwin. The Kerwin Ballet Theater, as his company came to be known, performed all around the area in the summers, including at Music Under the Stars and in summer musicals performed in Toledo and surrounding communities. The dancers loved it and loved being together. They learned so much at the school and in the company. Kerwin said of Woodward, "it was an arts school within a public school, and it was amazing how Sam pulled this all off. It was magic. The energy was so good; everyone was having such a good time and it was so energizing. It was the time of my life." Sam served as the musical director of the Kerwin Ballet Theater until the early 1970s, when Bud left Toledo, having been recruited to teach ballet at Butler University in Indianapolis, Indiana.

I had already started on violin and in ballet when Sam came to address my seventh grade class about the band. He was so positive and upbeat that I decided I wanted to join the band, which I did as a freshman. Sam encouraged me to continue violin and dancing too. I wanted to play flute, but there were already many flutes. Mr. Szor suggested trumpet, so I learned to play trumpet and later became a majorette. As a majorette, I had ballet classes with Bud, which led me to switch to his studio and become a part of his company.

My experiences at Woodward opened the door to things I had never been exposed to before—classical music, Broadway shows, such creativity. I remember Sam taking some of us to see "No Strings" with Diahann Carroll and Richard Kiley in the opening production at the Fischer theater in Detroit, and also to see "Oklahoma" at the Huron Playhouse; (Kerwin) took us to Detroit to see matinee performances of the Bolshoi and Moiseyev Dance Companies on several occasions.

I would play Broadway music on my record player until I wore out the grooves. I think I knew every verse of most of the songs! Our football shows were different from all the other bands. I remember I could not wait for summer band camp to start because we had so much fun and got so much encouragement and positive reinforcement. Being involved in the broadway shows brought out talent in me I didn't know I had.

In 1963 the band did a recording of the Woodward Fight Song and Alma Mater. Sam had the fight song arranged by Jerry Bilik, an arranger from U of M and it was really great. The other side of the 45 was the Woodward jazz combo. Sam and Bud Kerwin changed my life. Those were such great years!

Karen Benson Werner
Woodward High School, Class of 1964

The Woodward Extravaganza started in the days of Danny Thomas, the pride of Woodward High School, and was handed down to such stars as Paul White and Jameel Farah (aka Jamie Farr). For the first five years Sam was at Woodward, the Extrav as it was fondly called, was produced as a variety show. They were different from a usual variety shows however, in that there were story lines, each of which was written by Sam. The shows had a cast and an orchestra, and featured the talents of many students. Sam wrote arrangements and some original tunes for these productions. Some of them include: Ups and Downs (1952-53); Depressed Accelerator (1955-56); and To Lift or to Lean (1956-57).

After 1957 the Extravaganzas shifted to productions of Broadway shows. The shows picked were all big dance shows since the ballet/dance program had taken off and there was considerable talent available.

Kerwin, of course, served as the choreographer. Sam coached the singers, put together the orchestra—which was made up of Woodward students and members of the community where needed—and recruited assistance with all the other jobs that needed to be done. With his engaging personality, Sam was able to recruit students to chair and serve on such committees as Program Art and Design, Programs, Ticket and Finance, Backstage, Sound, Refreshments, Scenery, Stage Manager, Usherettes, Lighting, Properties, Patrons, Publicity, Scenery Construction, and Program Sales. In the final program of 1963, there were also fourteen Woodward faculty listed as assistants for the Extravaganza production. Because of Sam's ability to engage other people, these productions had come to involve the entire school and community.

Sam was Woodward High School, and that's what I've always aspired to be in all my years as a college teacher and fifteen years as president/chancellor of colleges from Kentucky to California. He brought his enthusiasm, intellect, good cheer, joy, can-do attitude to everything he touched. He made a difference in so many of our lives. I was just a skinny kid from Appalachia at Woodward, and I earned a Ph.D. from The Ohio State University and was chancellor of a California college with 40,000 students. Like Sam, I've always been interested in the power of the performing arts and performed a play I wrote about Hispanic women at colleges/universities/conferences from California to D.C. I say this not to brag, but to say that Woodward changed my life.
Vivian Bowling Blevins
Woodward High School, Class of 1956

Tom Bollin, Woodward High School class of 1959, was in the band and involved in the Extravs, serving as student director his senior year. That was the beginning of long professional relationship for Sam, Kerwin, and Bollin. Bollin served as technical director or director of all the Extravaganzas during Sam's tenure at Woodward from 1959 on. Following Sam's departure from Woodward, the three worked together on many other productions. Bollin would go on to become an educator, school principal, and later school superintendent.

Although Sam's major instrument was bassoon, he was proficient on all the instruments and gave private lessons in addition to his responsibilities at Woodward. I remember taking trumpet lessons from him in the summers. He didn't follow any old rules about teaching. He talked to us instead of lecturing; he talked about excellence and constantly showed us examples of excellence. He talked about what excellence was, life lessons and how to be. Some of those life lessons included learning to appreciate others, learning about practical applications of courage, learning about how important values are to the way we lead our lives and learning that while we can do lots of things alone in this world, the most beautiful music is created when we work in ensemble with others. He kept upping the ante to make kids grow. And he taught that we had to work, we had to learn our trade, whatever it might be, as evidenced by his signing of high school students' yearbooks with only one word: "'Practice' S.P. Szor."

The set for "The Telephone Hour" from Woodward's production of *Bye Bye Birdie*, that was purchased by the University of Michigan.

He didn't really believe in grades. He gave all the students in band an A. In later years I asked about that and he said it was a reward for all the time, lessons, and effort they put into the band. His style had the potential for becoming chaotic, but it never did.

Tom Bollin
Woodward High School, Class of 1959

On the occasion of his induction into the Woodward Hall of Fame, Bollin reflected on his Woodward years and wrote: "the individual who had the most profound effect on me was Sam Szor. He was so much more than a band director. He profoundly influenced my life through his daily speeches in band about excellence, creativity, and all aspects of the arts. Sam showed all of us how to work hard if we wanted to make an impact. We all became part of something important when we joined his band, and we would be changed for the better as people for having had the experience."

The Broadway musicals produced by Sam while at Woodward include: *Girl Crazy* (1958), *Guys and Dolls* (1959), *Pajama Game* (1960), *Bells are Ringing* (1961), *Bye Bye Birdie* (1962), and *The Music Man* (1963). "The Telephone Hour" set from *Bye Bye Birdie* was so impressive that it was purchased by the University of Michigan following completion of the performances at Woodward. The sets for the Extravs were built by students and fathers. Terry Werner, Woodward High School class of 1962, recalled "The Telephone Hour" set was built by himself and three other students and one of the student's fathers. The father donated all the materials, supplied the welding materials, and allowed the students to do some of the welding. They had to sneak into the building at night to get it done, to use the machine shop and the wood shop. Two of the students used to stand lookout for the school maintenance person so he would not hear them using all the saws and sanders. Students also painted the sets.

Scenes from Woodward's production of *Pajama Game*. Dancers perform "Once a Year Day," (bottom) and "Steam Heat" (right).

Sam taught me everything about "show" business, including "know your audience." I was a second violinist but attended football games with the marching band. Majorettes were expected to be competent in dance—study modern ballet with Bud Kerwin—and in putting on a show. The halftime shows were contemporary; for instance, for Camelot, the band dressed in tights—black on one leg, white on the other—under a tunic top with the majorettes in twelfth century gowns. I saw him take "problem" kids and put them on the stage—he was creative, most kind, and absolutely mined talent. A real "music man" and human being.

Phillip Kaufman
Woodward High School, Class of 1964

Along with the musical *The Music Man* in 1963, Sam and Kerwin prepared what they called the Woodward High School Opera and Ballet Workshops. The Opera Workshop presented the Gian-Carlo Menotti opera, *The Telephone*, and the Ballet Workshop performed *Billy the Kid*, a ballet based on the American legend of Billy the Kid. Both were quite ambitious undertakings. Written in program for *The Music Man* was the following:

Mr. Szor's fierce dedication to a professional—indeed, to a veritable perfectionist standard of performance and the extraordinary response this dedication evokes from his admiring students have enhanced Woodward's reputation to such an extent that we recently received a unique compliment from the conductor of the Toledo Orchestra. Mr. Joseph Hawthorne remarked on our stage that only one other high school in the nation has attempted as ambitious a production as the twin bill, *Billy the Kid* and *The Telephone* presented here March 7, 1963.

This collaboration between Sam and Kerwin at Woodward High School provided a great foundation and preparation for those who wanted to continue in the arts. A number of Sam's students did, in fact, pursue their interest in the arts and realized great success.

Even with his mushrooming responsibilities at Woodward, Sam

Sam, shortly after being named director of Music Under the Stars.

took on a variety of other jobs throughout Toledo's musical community. By 1959 Sam was choir director of the Broadway United Methodist Church, director of Music Under the Stars, was playing second bassoon in the Toledo Symphony Orchestra, and had been named the conductor of the Toledo Choral Society. In addition to his work at Woodward and associated schools, Sam also taught private lessons and conducted the Putnam County music festival in 1961.

While teaching at Woodward, Sam returned to University of Michigan to work on his Masters degree. An unpleasant memory from his continuing education at U of M made Sam laugh years later. He had finished all of the requirements, or so he thought, to graduate with his Master of Music Education degree. When speaking with his advisor about graduation, Sam was told he could not graduate because he was short one class: "Introduction to Graduate Studies." Sam couldn't believe it, but had to return the next summer to complete the introductory course and finally get his advanced degree in August of 1958.

There was so much talent among the Woodward students that Sam nurtured. Several students recalled times after school when Sam would get out his saxophone and jam with them. That's when they learned to start to improvise, and several students, including Dick Martin, were already playing professional gigs while in high school.

Some of us, including me, gave Sam some gray hair when we were in school. I was first trumpet in the band which is an important position. One day we were marching in a parade. There was a small store on the corner and three of us trumpets decided we could run into the store to get a soda and be back before the band started to play again. We didn't make it—the band started to play and there were no first trumpets. Sam turned the whole band around and marched it back to the store while he ran inside to pull us out. We knew we were in big trouble. I think we were suspended for a time.

Another time it was just a couple weeks before the Extravaganza and I decided I was going to go to Florida for a week, missing important rehearsals. Sam was furious and gave the first trumpet book to another guy. The other trumpet player was much younger and not ready however, so he eventually gave it back to me. I also remember the time we were going outside to practice marching. It was cold out and Sam was late getting out to the field because of a call or something. By the time he arrived, we had a bon fire going on the field—the fire material being our band music! Having spent my whole professional life as a music teacher, I look back on those high school years and wonder how he ever put up with the shenanigans we pulled.

In reflecting back on my memories of Sam on a more serious note however, many recollections come to mind. He was a great influence on me musically and personally. In August of 1957, as I was about to enter my freshman year of high school at Woodward, my father was killed in an auto accident. My dad and I were both trumpet players. On my first day of band, Sam and all the band members welcomed me enthusiastically. I felt so well received that day.

Sam recognized that I was a pretty good player and wanted to encourage me to continue my musical growth, so Sam would go out of his way to pick me up in the mornings before school. I would get extra practice before school both with the band music as well as "jamming" with other talented players which sometimes included Sam on sax or up-right bass. What an experience that was, not only learning how to improvise but also introducing me to lifelong friends.

Sam challenged us musically in concert band with the latest band arrangements, which were often very difficult. Sam directed our Extravaganzas each year which gave me experience of playing Broadway musicals. This exposure helped prepare me to play professional Broadway shows in Louisville which I did for many years. In addition, he gave me the opportunity to play Music Under the Stars each summer.

It was during those years in high school and college that Sam inspired me to major in music and become a band director, which I did for over 35 years. I also continued to play professionally as I previously mentioned in Broadway touring shows, local big bands, circuses, ice shows, performances with the Louisville Orchestra and fronting my own Dixieland band. What an influence Sam was in preparing me for all of this. Not only was Sam a wonderful teacher, I treasured him as a good friend. Although I moved to Louisville in the 60s, whenever I would get back to Toledo, I would always take time for a visit with Sam.

Dick Martin
Woodward High School, Class of 1963

Sam with his parents, Samuel and Mary.

Sam's older son, Tom, assembled a collection of wonderful photographs documenting Sam's years at Woodward. Taken by professional photographer Bill Hartough, the photographs are from band shows, Extravaganzas, and Kerwin ballets. These photos are a testament to the professional quality of these productions and the talent and dedication of everyone involved. The photos were first exhibited at the main branch of the Toledo-Lucas County Public Library in 2016. They can be found online, in the library's digital collections section by searching for "Sam Szor Collection."

Dan Duvendack went to DeVilbiss high school but had a presence at Woodward because his father was the principal when Sam was hired. He used to sit in with the band during rehearsals on occasion, and he began teaching at Woodward in 1959. He recalled a Woodward-DeVilbiss football game where the Woodward drum major came out and dazzled the crowd. It turned out the regular drum major was ill, so Sam put on the uniform and led the band that night. This was not unusual for Sam—he was willing to do whatever was necessary to get the job done.

The Woodward High School marching band, around 1962, with more than 100 members.

Tom Treece met Sam through private lessons. Even though he didn't attend Woodward, he was around a lot there, at The University of Toledo, and at Music Under the Stars. He sometimes sat in with the bands and helped out in a lot of ways, including building the risers for Music Under the Stars. He said he learned so much from Sam, especially how to deal with people. "Sam would size up students and the situation quickly and know exactly what to do," Treece said. "He could get people to do things

A sketch of Sam by Diana Attie from the 1963 Woodward High School yearbook, The Sage.

no one else could. I have used techniques I learned from Sam my whole life, especially how to use humor to make obvious points. (Sam was well known for his humor and did use it effectively.) Sam always stood up for students and helped a lot of people."

Sam's last Woodward Extravaganza was *The Music Man* in the spring of 1963, as he had accepted a position at Toledo University starting later that year. The school honored its outgoing director in the *The Music Man* program:

> If anyone qualifies for the title of "Music Man of Toledo," it is certainly Mr. Samuel P. Szor who "knows the territory" intimately. There cannot be any phase of Toledo musical life— from Brubeck jazz to Bach chorales—that this young musician (spelled MAGICIAN) has not touched with his baton-wand. Like the Pied Piper, he has cast the spell of his infectious enthusiasm over Woodward's band and orchestra for 11 years and where he has led, they have followed. In 1952 the Woodward Band had about 15 members; today it has over 100.

In addition to his amazing musical talents, this versatile young man brings a fine intellectual background, an inexhaustible amount of general information, and a deep respect for the academic curriculum as gifts to inspire all the boys and girls with whom he comes in contact. His habitual relaxed grin, his matchless humor, his unfailing courtesy and consideration for others, even when plagued inwardly with a multitude of demanding details, coupled with his unparalleled generosity in the use of his time and talents, have endeared him to the whole staff. All Woodward claims Sam—the Band Room isn't big enough to hold him! … Woodward High School's banners will fly higher and more proudly because, for an unforgettable interval, two of our chief colorbearers were Robert E. Rettig (principal) and Samuel P. Szor."

By Sam's own account, his years at Woodward were a fantastic ride. The talent of the students and what he was able to accomplish with them while there, with immense support of the school, the parents, and the community, was nothing short of amazing. His time in the collegiate setting would be a study in contrasts. Sam would continue to incubate, nurture, and grow various musical programs; however, his efforts would be met with a mixture of appreciation and disdain.

Chapter 4
The University of Toledo

Having left the very supportive environment of Woodward High School "against the advice of some of the city's best advisers," according an article in the *Toledo Blade*, Sam started his career at The University of Toledo on July 1, 1963, as an assistant professor of music. In his Morning After column in the April 15, 1963 edition of the *Toledo Times*, Jim MacDonald reported on the integral role Sam was to play in the university's plans to expand the institution's music programs:

Szor To Add Swinging Sparkle To TU games

There'll be some real swinging times next fall at the Glass Bowl. This I can promise you.

I know little of Frank Lauterbur, the University of Toledo's new head football coach. And it is impossible at this time to predict how well the Rocket gridders will do. But, TU will provide some excellent pre-game and halftime entertainment.

In all the furor of hiring a new football coach, maybe there are those who missed the announcement of a new marching band coach being named at TU.

Officials refer to him as a director, but Sam Szor does as much planning, practicing and, yes, even scouting as any football coach in this area.

I got to know Sam when he was directing the Woodward

High School band, a post he gave up to take the position at TU. His Woodward bands were among the best in the state.

TU has never had an outstanding marching band and last fall had none. Szor will change this sad situation … Szor, who plans to field an 80-man marching band, is already busily engaged in recruiting.

Sam was to spend the summer recruiting and training 80 students to resurrect the school's marching band in time for football season that year. Sam was also tasked with building a "strong 50-piece orchestra for a debut in an all-Bach concert" that fall, in addition to organizing a summer music program for high school students to start the following year. MacDonald's column also details Sam's extensive involvement

in other Toledo area musical endeavors at the time. MacDonald notes Sam "has been the director of the Toledo Choral Society and also each summer conducts the 'Music Under the Stars' programs at the zoo. In addition, he plays the bassoon in the Toledo Orchestra."

Sam had a lot on his plate, but he also had big ideas. He worked hard at recruiting that first summer. A $50 stipend for members of the marching band

Sam "on the horn" in his UT office.

enticed good student musicians—some of whom followed him from Woodward—who could have been making money at professional jobs rather than playing in the marching band. The money, plus Sam's engaging personality were enough to successfully recruit them for the band.

In an article in the September 20, 1963 edition of the university's student newspaper *The Collegian*, Sam said the debut performance of the 64-member marching band would feature an "Early Bird Show" that would be rehearsals of the band beginning about an hour before game time for the benefit of early arrivals at night games. Prior to the start of home games, the band would march across campus to the Glass Bowl, playing as it marched. Sam also planned a "four- to six-minute show prior to playing the National Anthem at each game, plus appropriate music as the starting lineups are introduced by having the players run through the goal posts to the center of the field." But Sam wasn't done. According to the article, "Each Rocket touchdown and extra point will be celebrated by a musical arrangement. Besides the halftime show, there will be a special performance to entertain fans as they are leaving the Glass Bowl."

The Rocket marching band made its debut at the first home game of the season, on September 28, 1963, when the Rockets hosted Villanova. The band's program for that night was titled "Our Coming Out Party," and featured military, high step, and dancing routines to music from "Strike Up the Band," "Everything's Coming Up Roses," and "Ballin the Jack," plus a formation to "Off We Go Into the Wild Blue Yonder." The post-game show featured Gershwin's "I Got Rhythm." Sam had secured the services of fellow U of M graduate and nationally-known musical arranger Jerry H. Bilik to write special arrangements for the marching band.

The band was very well received by the community during the 1963 football season. It was the topic of the cover story of the *Toledo Blade's* Sunday Magazine on November 10, 1963. "The Miracle on Bancroft Street," by Seymour Rothman, included many photos and a sub-title proclaiming, "From no band's land to biggest and best band in the history of the University of Toledo—that's Sam Szor's success story." The article chronicled Sam's process in recruiting and his persuasiveness in getting things done. Rothman described band rehearsals and how they had always been on the sixth floor of University Hall. Sam said, "have you ever carried a sousaphone up six flights of stairs or tried to squeeze one into a small and crowded elevator?" This argument won Sam some space in temporary barracks between University Hall and the Student Union for a band room. He similarly tackled and solved issues of a practice field, more band instruments, and rehearsal time. Steve Worshtil, a band member and one of Sam's students from Woodward, was a new source for band arrangements. Former students recall crowds stayed on after football games to listen to the band's postgame shows because the music was so good—contemporary charts, many arranged by Worshtil.

The Miracle On Bancroft Street

From no band's land to biggest
and best band in the history of the University of Toledo
—that's Sam Szor's success story

By SEYMOUR ROTHMAN
Blade Staff Writer

SAM SZOR would make a great football coach—if he knew anything about football.

(Please Turn To Page 6)

The first page of the Sunday Magazine article about Sam and the University of Toledo band that appeared in the November 10, 1963 edition of the *The Blade*.

An article in the October 11, 1963 edition of *The Collegian*, detailed Sam's efforts to start a school orchestra. Sam was able to recruit 42 students—22 of whom played in the marching band—to join the orchestra. The music department had to purchase seven additional string instruments for the orchestra. The orchestra's first concert was in February 1964. It performed Beethoven, *Symphony No. 1 in C Major* and Schubert, *Symphony No.5 in B♭ Major*. Their efforts were well-received, according to an article in the February 28, 1964 edition of *The Collegian*:

> Mr. Wallace Martin, assistant professor of English stated, "The concert was a remarkable improvement over previous years. Mr. Szor deserves our gratitude for the work he has done." Dr. Michael Manheim head of the humanities division, termed the performance, "Splendid! The tone was excellent and it compares most favorably with other college orchestras I have heard." Dean Jerome Kloucek, of the College of Arts and Sciences said, "Mr. Szor certainly has a well-disciplined unit which brought out a good interpretation of the pieces," and Mr. Arthur Winsor, instructor in music, thought that the concert, which he termed "very impressive" suggests that "the future of the orchestra is very secure."

Sam participated in a number of other programs in the spring of his first year at the university, including: conducting the band for the Lucas County Music Festival held April 7, 1964 in the Field House; Arts Festival week sponsored by the Student Union Board for a week in April 1964 with Sam conducting the Concert Band during a concert on April 23 and the University of Toledo Orchestra for the Kerwin Ballet Theater performance of "Apollo" and "Opus Jazz" for An Evening of Ballet on April 24; and the University Orchestra and choir concert on May 17, 1964 of Mozart *Overture to The Magic Flute*, his *Eine Kleine Nachtmusik* and excerpts from Mozart's *Requiem*. Sam also organized the university's Summer School of Music for high school students from June 15 to July

19, 1964. In addition to his band and orchestra responsibilities, Sam taught music theory and played in the University Woodwind Trio. He used to tell the story of preparing for the music theory class and how the lesson plan he prepared for the first class lasted him almost the whole first semester.

His second year at the university was more of the same. Sam continued to build the marching and concert bands and orchestra, presenting concerts with all ensembles, teaching music theory, and playing in the university's Woodwind Trio. Recruiting more musicians was always high on his priority list. To aid in his recruitment efforts, Sam took the band out to surrounding schools to play and would invite high school students to visit the university. According to former students, the band often played arrangements of popular tunes of the day during school tours, to capture the interest of the high school students. In addition to his other responsibilities, he joined with the theater department to be the musical director for productions they were presenting. These included Bertolt Brecht and Kurt Weil's *Three Penny Opera* in 1964, the comedy *Little Mary Sunshine* in 1965 directed by Al Gordon, *Oh What a Lovely War* directed by Bernard Coyne in 1966, and Peter Weiss's *The Persecution and Assassination of Jean-Paul Marat as Performed by the Inmates of the Asylum of Charenton Under the Direction of Marquis de Sade* in 1968.

Concert band programs from 1966 and 1967 showed substantial repertoire being presented—pieces by such composers as Massenet, Rachmaninoff, Verdi, Mozart, Stravinsky, Dvorak, Copland, and the like. Despite everything he was doing, there were a number of obstacles placed in his way and Sam felt a huge lack of support from the music department. As a result, in September 1966 Sam wrote a letter to Dr. Jesse Long, the University's Executive Vice President, stating he felt his effectiveness as an educator was being hampered because of unwarranted negative attitude toward him and his program from

Sam promoting tryouts for *Oh What A Lovely War*.

the Music Department and College of Arts and Sciences. He asked to have the band program transferred to the College of Education. John Beddoes, a band member who had followed Sam from Woodward to the university, witnessed what was going on first-hand.

Sam immediately started rebuilding a program that was faltering and weak. He was often frustrated by a music department that was entrenched and obstructive. Of course, part of the cause of the marching band's sorry state was the low priority it had within the department. The competition within the Music Department for a piece of the limited budget didn't allow for a lot of support for the Marching Band. Sam's enthusiastic efforts to finance improvements and growth in the band were not all that welcome. He was not treated well by many in the department. Despite all the frustration, Sam never stopped working at it and never let his public face show how angry he really was.

John Beddoes
Woodward High School, Class of 1963

Despite these challenges, Sam continued to do his work. In 1967 he was selected to direct the Cattaragus County, New York All-County Band in Portville, New York, bringing recognition to the university and it's music program. He also conducted the Monroe County Band Festival in Ida, Michigan in 1964, the Williams County All-County band music festivals in 1967 and 1969, the Southwest Michigan District 6 All-Star Band in Bridgman, Michigan in 1970, and the Watervliet School Bands in April of 1970.

In 1967 Sam resigned as assistant professor of music and was named director of University Bands—marching and concert—under the division of Student Services. According to an article in the October 20, 1967 edition of the university's in-house newsletter, Dr. Lancelot Thompson, dean of student services, said:

> Mr. Szor's work with student musical groups is properly a function of the student activities program of the University of Toledo. …. Consequently, it is agreeable with him, the music department, and the division of student services to place the University bands within expanding student services program. I believe it will permit Mr. Szor to do more effective recruiting and will stimulate the growth of the bands.

According to the same article, the marching band was the largest in the school's history with 80 members plus alternates, twirlers, and a drum major. In addition, the Rock-ets, a group of girls who danced along when the band performed had also been added.

An article in a December 1967 edition of the *Toledo Times* reported Sam was also starting a stage band that rehearsed on Tuesdays and a

THE UNIVERSITY OF TOLEDO MARCHING BAND

SAMUEL P. SZOR, Director of Bands

STEVE WORSHTIL, Arranger   **BUD KERWIN, Choreographer**

You Are Invited To Join

★ NEW UNIFORMS

★ UNIQUE MUSICAL ARRANGEMENTS

★ STUNNING MARCHING MANEUVERS

★ ONE HOUR CREDIT (No fee)

★ EIGHT DANCING GIRLS

★ "LEROY"

TRY-OUTS:
Monday, September 23, 1968 — 9:00 A.M. — Student Union, Room 216

FIRST REHEARSAL:
Monday, September 23, 1968 — 2:00 P.M. — Student Union, Room 216

For Further Information: The University of Toledo Bands
Student Union Building, Room 321, Phone 531-5711, Ext. 459

SA 40 968 5C

After resigning as assistant professor of music, Sam was named director of University Bands, which had been transferred to the division of Student Services. He continued his recruitment efforts in his new position.

Student Union Choir that rehearsed on Mondays, Wednesdays, and Fridays, both of which were open to all students enrolled at the university. In addition to his band and choir responsibilities, in May 1968, the Student Union Board produced, under the direction of Sam, *How to Succeed in Business Without Really Trying*. Stage direction was done by Tom Bollin and choreography by Bud Kerwin. Following its three-day run, Sam received a letter from Dean Thompson complementing Sam and the cast for "the splendid performance of the first Musicale to be put on by the University, solely run by the Student Union Board."

"I hope the tradition is just starting for programs of this kind in the future," Thompson's letter continued. "The audience, as I sat watching the performance, really enjoyed themselves, and I think this kind of enjoyment is wholesome for the entire University community. Again, thank you for providing an enjoyable weekend."

At the end of May of the same year, *Ray and the Gospel Singer*, a comic opera, music written by local composer Elizabeth Gould and libretto by local Eugene Hochman, was also presented in the university's Doermann Theater, under the direction of Bollin, with Sam as the music director. The production was a collaborative effort under the auspices of the Student Union Board, division of adult and continuing education, and the department of music.

I had the wonderful good fortune to be one of Sam's students at Woodward and the University of Toledo. He was a role model for living life energetically and intelligently, for hearing the music and for loving people. He was and still is my hero.

Marie Reuter Troxell
Woodward High School, Class of 1962

Sam continued to visit area schools in his efforts to recruit students for the marching band and the Noon-Time Singers, the choir he started in student activities. On one day alone in February 1969, the band's schedule included performances at three area high schools: Rossford, Libbey, and St. Francis. On this tour, the band and choir performed popular tunes of the day such as "Do You Know the Way to San Jose," "Mercy, Mercy, Mercy," and "Watermelon Man." This kind of programming was not viewed favorably by UT's music department. Even in Student Services there were still objections to Sam's teaching methods and programs from the music department.

In May 1969, Noel L. Leathers, then Dean of the College of Arts and Sciences, announced a new faculty member, Kenley Inglefield, was going to lead UT's instrumental music education program and would be responsible for all bands and music organization within the department and the academic program. In his memo, Leathers said UT would "clearly differentiate between music education and music entertainment."

"It has been our failure to clearly understand and acknowledge this difference that has caused so much hard feeling in the past," the memo continued. "Mr. Szor in his function as director of musical activities in the student activities field clearly aims at providing entertainment. I can personally attest after yesterday that he does this job extremely well. The program of instrumental music education, however, is not geared to entertain but to prepare our students to go out upon graduation into our public schools and provide educational music experiences. Therefore, their education on this campus must include serious and thorough preparation if they are to do the job. ... I would also strongly recommend that Mr. Szor continue in the field of music entertainment and service to the University and its students as well as the community. This division of labor should eliminate such animosity that has heretofore marked this area."

In light of his many accomplishments and successes at the University, this was a hard pill to swallow. That summer Sam was named associate director of student activities responsible for supervision of Student Union Board, development of programs involving individual participation by students, and coordination of Homecoming and Winter and Spring weekends. One of the new activities he produced while in this role was a musical review that featured talent from the football team, the Interfraternity Council, Panhellenic Council, Residence Hall Association, independents, faculty and staff. Proceeds from the show went to the Martin Luther King, Jr. Memorial Scholarship Fund.

In contrast to the music department faculty, Sam's untiring efforts did not go unrecognized by the students. In 1970, the University's yearbook, The Blockhouse, was dedicated to him with a full-page photo and this paragraph:

> To Sam Szor, To many people many things: a friend, an advisor, a musician. His enthusiasm is contagious, his friendship is invaluable. To Mr. Szor, a friend who never stoops to talk on the student's level but lets you speak to him on his, the staff of the Blockhouse dedicates "The University Community."

While Sam's accomplishments at UT were impressive—from resurrecting a failing marching band program to adding additional musical and performing arts opportunities for students—he had grown weary of other aspects of working in a collegiate setting. Sam left the University in 1973 to return to teaching music full-time at his high school alma mater, Waite High School.

Chapter 5
Waite High School

Building a band program was once again the top of Sam's to do list when he took the position at Waite High School in August 1973. He had little time to recruit and develop high school musicians before football season started. Sam only had about 40 students in band his first year. Also during this time—from 1973 to 1976—area high school bands would participate in an annual marching band festival. Each band would present a show to the public. Despite the small numbers—at least for a high school band—Sam was not about to let his beloved Waite High School be outdone.

To face off against other schools with large established programs, he had to dig deep into his creative mind. Sam hired Steve Worshtil, who had written arrangements for the UT band, to write arrangements for a rock 'n roll Sha-na-na inspired show for the Waite band to perform the first year. To stand out against all the other bands, Waite band members abandoned their traditional uniform in favor of rolled up blue jeans, white t-shirts, and slicked back hair for the boys, and similar outfits with bobby socks and saddle shoes for the girls. They played such tunes as "At the Hop" and "Rock Around the Clock" to the crowd's delight.

Sam continued to recruit for the band the following school year. The band's show for the marching band festival that year was a Beatles show featuring Worshtil's arrangements of "Sgt. Pepper's Lonely Hearts Club Band" and "My Sweet Lord." Again, their performance was very well received by the audience. As he had done at both Woodward and

UT, now at Waite, Sam again called on his tried and tested strategy of providing students with as many opportunities to perform as possible. To that end, he took eighteen band students (members of the popular jazz band he had also started at Waite) to Watervliet, Michigan to give a concert.

When I think of high school, the first thing that pops into my head is always band and Sam Szor. Sam was able to put both my interest in music and art to good use over those 4 years at Waite and beyond. Sam

The Waite band tap dancing on pieces of Masonite.

found a way to find hidden talent in people and bring it to light. He was able to recruit students to join the band who didn't necessarily have a background on the instrument he was assigning them, but he knew they'd be good for the group. He just kept going and moving forward. Somehow he found the instruments needed, the kids to play them, and the band grew in number and skill. The band could see the positive results in themselves and in the reaction of the audience and community. I was hooked!

Our band shows included a themed program of music plus costumes. I remember costumes for a '50s show, Beatles show, Mickey Mouse Club show, and George M. Cohan show. The Cohan show was particularly memorable since all the band members had to learn how to tap dance. We all had tap shoes and our own 2x4 sheet of Masonite to dance on as we played. Step, Shuffle, Ball Change! One specific memory I have of the jazz band is playing in Watervliet. I believe it was one of the first times the jazz band had played out because I remember being anxious about a solo. The piece was going well, the solo was getting closer and all of the sudden here's Sam with a microphone right in front of my saxophone! I had never heard myself play over a mic before. I was scared and exhilarated at the same time. If he had told me ahead of time that he was going to mic the solos, I would have been a nervous wreck. Good call on the surprise!

I'll always appreciate the passion and enthusiasm that Sam brought to the Waite Band Program. He ignited in me a passion for music that continues to evolve. He showed me musical theater, which is something I still love. He taught me that I could do more than I thought I could, and for that I'm forever thankful. He wasn't only my teacher, but a dear friend that could always make me laugh (or groan) with a corny joke. I feel blessed that I was able to be his student and friend.

Diane Lamberton Spahr
Waite High School, Class of 1977

By the start of the 1975-76 school year, Sam's third year at Waite, students had become believers in the band, swelling its ranks to more than 100 members. That year they did a Disney show for the marching band festival and were invited by Congressman Ludlow Ashley to play in Washington D.C. as part of the nation's Bicentennial Salute. They were one of only four bands from Ohio to be chosen. A photo of the band on the front steps of the U.S. Capitol was featured on the front page of the Sunday, March 27, 1976 edition of the *Toledo Blade*. The caption read: "The Waite High School band performed Friday in Washington. The Waite group was the first of several Ohio bands to play in the District of Columbia's bicentennial salute to Ohio, 'because it is the best band in Ohio,' Congressman Thomas L. Ashley said." Also in 1976, Sam produced and was musical director for the Feather Waite Follies, a variety show for students called *Yankee Doodle*. It was a show in two acts with five scenes: the Revolutionary War, the Civil War, World War I,

The Waite band on the steps of the U.S. Capitol in 1976.

World War II, and Post War. Soon after his arrival at Waite, Sam began work to have the auditorium stage made into a thrust proscenium—where the stage extends into the audience—so that they would be able to use it for shows. The Feather Waite Follies was the first production on the new stage.

I believe starting our freshman year at Waite High School, I as a student and Sam as the band director, provided great opportunities. I had no idea what to expect, and he had no limitations around what would be expected. I could read music as a result of piano lessons and having played the oboe the previous two years. However, when I met Sam prior to the start of summer band rehearsals, I asked if I could play the drums. Little did I realize at the time that his willingness to provide that opportunity would form the foundation for building a great personal and professional relationship with Sam and his family.

The experiences he provided the next four years were unbelievable. Putting together the jazz band and the performances and competitions, marching band trip to Washington D.C. with performances at many of the national monuments, 100+ piece tap dancing band with "BYOB" (Bring Your Own Board). Each band member carried their own dancing surface along with their instrument onto the field to provide dancing and musical performances at half-time shows and other performances. We probably didn't realize it at the time, but the experiences we shared under Sam's direction and guidance would be some of the most educational and valuable experiences of our high school careers.

After high school and for years to come, I had the privilege to continue performing with "Mr. Music." I performed under his baton with the Music Under the Stars Concert Band, Perrysburg Symphony Orchestra, Toledo Choral Society, First Congregational Church, and numerous other performance opportunities. I owe a lot to Sam. His willingness to believe in me and take a chance on my musical abilities 45 years ago has allowed me to enjoy music and continue preforming. I feel blessed to have been a small part of the Sam Szor legacy.

Mike Spahr
Waite High School, Class of 1977

Just like his years at Woodward, Sam had a nontraditional approach to his teaching and recruiting at Waite. An article about the Waite band published in the Thursday, November 30, 1978 edition of the *Oregon News* opined:

> Waite High School's band is definitely entertaining, probably more so than any other. When they march onto the field, it's exciting—you never know what to expect. It could be anything from a rock concert to a song-and-dance routine. Their reputation is well established.

Sam discussed how he built another exceptional program when many students had little to no experience. "In a situation where there is little involvement in private training (lessons), except for baton twirling, one must be practical in expectations ... Few of the band members own instruments, so high interest through the music played must be generated," he told the newspaper. Sam found a variety of ways to open his student's eyes to music:

> "Take whatever is popular. If I showed you a score to 'Reminiscin'" it would frighten you. Look at those rhythms—that's Bartok." He pulled out a baritone part for "Boogie-oogie-oogie." "That's Vivaldi," he said. So the band plays radio music.
>
> "That's all they hear," Szor explained. And while it doesn't make for much versatility, where the so-called classics are concerned, Szor teaches it, emphasizing the proper rhythms and hopes "they transfer that discipline to other music," he said.

When it came to selecting music for the band, Sam took students' tastes into consideration every time. He would ask band members what they wanted to play. "They make the judgement, and then have a very strong commitment. And what's coming from all of this? We have more and more kids who want to do serious music," he said.

Sam was truly a great teacher in every sense of the word, he instilled the love of music, respect for your fellow man, he taught with passion and drive, and he didn't just expect the best, he commanded it and most of us willingly gave it…true genius and irreplaceable!

Beth Swartz O'Shea
Waite High School, Class of 1977

Over the next seven years, the band continued to make its mark on the Toledo area for its creativity, musicianship, and visibility. In 1976-77 a flag corps was added to the band bringing its total to nearly 130 students, including the eight majorettes and twirler. The following school year the job of arranger for the band transitioned from Worshtil to Sam's son, Tom Szor. Most of the charts Tom wrote were top 40 tunes at the students' request. Some of the band's most significant shows between 1976 and 1984 included a Disney show, a show based on the Broadway musical *Annie*, a KISS show (every student researched and did

The Waite band dressed for "The Clown Show" in 1981. (Photo by Herral Long, courtesy *The Blade*).

his/her own makeup), a tap dance show (every band member learned to tap dance from East side dance instructor Shirley Brewer, and each had a 3x4 foot piece of Masonite they carried onto the football field to tap on), a Blues Brothers show, a Clown show based on the musical *Barnum*, and a show based on the musical *CATS*. Tom Lawson, Waite High School class of 1979, wrote Sam a note years later in which he said:

> Out of the blue I started to think about you today and I realized how much having you as a teacher meant to me in my younger days. You taught me not to be afraid to try anything, and to have the confidence to see it through. My band years were some of the most positive years of my life. They made me a better musician and person, and your influence continues to help me through my adult years. Thank you and with much love, Tom Lawson.

While Sam worked tirelessly to provide his students with a multitude of opportunities to perform, he also believed they would learn and grow if exposed to examples of excellence. During his tenure at Waite High School he took band members to see *A Chorus Line* at the Fisher theater in Detroit and to hear the Toledo Symphony Orchestra in the Peristyle of the Toledo Museum of Art. Sam also set up opportunities for the band to travel and perform in New York City and Toronto. In New York City they played at Martin Luther King High School and Lincoln Center and went to see the musical *42nd Street* on Broadway. In Toronto they played at Scarborough High School and toured the Ontario Science Center.

My band experience at Waite High School was remarkable in many ways, but as I thought about it, probably the greatest lesson I learned from Sam's teachings was to look at the big picture. I remember being very angry when I learned that everyone in the band got A's on their report cards. There were a lot of band members who didn't work as hard as me or play their instruments as well as I did. But through Sam's teachings, I finally realized that we are only as strong as our weakest link. It finally sunk in that for our band to be outstanding, my whole flute section (and all the sections) had to be really good; we were striving

The Waite band dressed for "The Blues Brother Show" (Photo courtesy *The Blade*).

to get an A as a unit. This realization has and continues to help me in my life. It took a lot of steps for me to get to that understanding, but I understand now that we must help everyone and each other, as everyone affects the big picture.

Aida Garcia Cardenas
Waite High School, Class of 1978

The football season for the 1977-78 school year was shortened due to a teachers' strike. Sam's workload was not lessened however, as he also assumed responsibility for the school's choir program that year, a duty he would perform until his retirement. From the band and choir, he could draw on talent to perform in school musicals, which of course was yet another program for which Sam was responsible. These included: *Guys and Dolls* (1977), *How to Succeed in Business without Really Trying* (1979), *Pajama Game* (1980), and *Bye Bye Birdie* (1981).

Sam was my high school music director, extreme perfectionist in charge, and my primary musical inspiration and musical mentor. We did theater shows in a school where there was not a theater department, and the other schools with massive programs and budgets used to come and be stupefied at what we did. I'm permanently stupefied! After my father died my freshman year in high school Sam grabbed me and filled me to overflowing with music of all kinds. I mean all kinds! He had a majestic incarnation and he'll be back to inflict his brilliance and goofy fun on countless others as a musical Bodhisattva. He'll be missed and not replaced!

Mark Danisovszky
Waite High School, Class of 1977

In keeping with Sam's belief that musicians need to perform frequently, band members could expect a packed schedule each year. The 1980-81 school year schedule is typical of each of his years at Waite:

Aug. 18	Marching Band rehearsals begin
Aug. 28	Meet the Team program in Stadium

Aug. 29	DeVilbiss Game
Sept. 3	School starts
Sept. 5	Macomber Game
Sept. 6	Cedar Point concert
Sept. 12	"Energy Brake" parade downtown (Toledo Edison)
Sept. 12	St. Francis Game
Sept. 19	Clay Game - Blues Brothers
Oct. 3	Homecoming Queen Coronation Ceremony (Fieldhouse)
Oct. 4	Homecoming Parade - Rogers Game Alumni Band pregame
Oct. 11	Libbey Homecoming Parade - Libbey Game
Oct. 16	Mondale rally - St. Stephen's
Oct. 18	St. John's Game
Oct. 22	Levis Square rally for school levy
Oct. 24	Woodville mall concert for school levy
Oct. 25	Bowsher Game
Oct. 29	Band Halloween Party
Nov. 1	University of Toledo Homecoming Parade Alumni Tent Concert (school levy) Toledo - Miami Post-game show - Blues Brothers
Nov. 2	Stritch Game Senior recognition - Senior march (campus) Senior party
Nov. 3	East side truck canvas (school levy) two trucks
Nov. 9	Old Newsboys' Association "Shoe Bowl" game
Dec. 5	Pep session in Field House (Stritch Game)
Dec. 6	East Toledo Christmas Parade
Dec. 10	St. John's Game (Basketball)
Dec. 12	Old Newsboys' Paper Sale (O-I Building)
Dec. 13	University of Toledo Centennial Hall (Detroit vs. Toledo)
Dec. 16	East Toledo elementary School Concerts East Side Central - Birmingham - Franklin - Navarre - Oakdale
Dec. 18	Waite Christmas Programs (auditorium)

Dec. 19	Boardroom at Administration Building - Christmas program
Dec. 19	Central Game (basketball)
Jan. 9	Woodward basketball game
Jan. 19	Clay-Waite Hockey (Sports Arena)
Jan. 21	Libbey Game (Girls basketball)
Jan. 23	Pep rally in Field House
Jan. 24	Waite Wrestling Tournament
Jan. 30	Scott basketball game
Feb. 3	Bowsher basketball game
Feb. 27	Faculty Feud (auditorium)
Feb. 28	Junior Achievement Trades Fair - Opening Ceremony
Mar. 1	All-County Choral Festival (peristyle)
Mar. 20-21	Rock-a-thon (Main Street)
Mar. 23	Waite Hockey (Sports Arena)
Mar. 28	Fruit sale
Apr. 15	Fairfield School P.T.A. concert
Apr. 30	Mexican-American Queen Coronation
May 5	North Central Evaluation
May 6	Toledo Symphony Orchestra percussion ensemble
May 9-12	New York Trip - concerts Martin Luther King HS and Lincoln Center
May 13	Toledo Symphony Orchestra - Woodwind quintet
May 20	Memorial Day Service (auditorium and monument)
May 21	The American Red Cross 100th Anniversary in Levis Square
May 29	*Bye, Bye Birdie* matinee
May 29-30	*Bye, Bye Birdie*
May 30	Memorial Service - Willow Cemetery Memorial Day Parade - downtown
Jun. 3	Band recognition program
Jun. 5	Commencement

In the fall of 1981 while driving his daughter Martha back to University of Michigan, he struck a horse one night on U.S. 23. He was off work for six weeks because of the injuries he sustained in the auto accident. His son, Tom, who was also a music educator, took over in his absence. Sam returned to teaching after recovering and continued on as always. Perhaps his time off gave him opportunity for reflection, and he subsequently decided he would retire in December 1983, after nearly 32 full years in the academic arena. An article in the December 1, 1983 edition of the *Toledo Blade* described the reaction to Sam's retirement. Students lamented his departure:

> "He takes into consideration that you are a separate person, not just a part of the band," Jodi Slaughterbeck, 15, a clarinet player, said. "He will take you aside separately if you are having trouble. He won't embarrass you."
>
> Joann Sparks, 15, another band member, said a lot of classmates were crying on Sam's last day, Wednesday, because they didn't want him to leave.

Parents shared students' feelings about his departure. One parent, Alice Horn, told *The Blade* three of her sons took band lessons from Sam and "she believes that he was an important figure in their lives." She also told *The Blade*:

> "All the boys have come back from time to time to talk with him," Mrs. Horn said. "I think that is the way most of the kids feel about him. I am sorry to see him leave. They are going to really miss him."
>
> She said Mr. Szor taught his students not only to play band instruments but to be musicians. He was willing to give help on instruments that fall outside the band ensemble, such as guitar.

Bettie Naugle, a member of the Waite Band Parents Association, went to school with Sam. Both were in the Waite High School band in 1948— she playing trumpet while he was drum major. Naugle said Sam "makes it exciting because he uses up-to-date, contemporary music that the kids are interested in … They like the idea they are putting on different shows. He's got a magnetism that he can get these kids together to perform the way they do … Yet he can be very tough. They know he expects the best of them, and they will come through."

On December 20, 1983, on the occasion of Sam's retirement, the Toledo City Council passed a resolution commending Sam for his years of service, describing him as:

> A prominent and innovative musician in the City of Toledo for over 30 years" who "has enriched the artistic life of Toledoans as a teacher in the high school and university level [who] has brought enjoyment to thousands of Toledoans as the conductor of the Music Under the Stars concert series since 1953; as an outstanding performer with various symphony and opera orchestras and quintets in the Northwestern Ohio area; and as the musical director and conductor of the Toledo Choral Society since 1958; and … the students and the music lovers of Toledo are indebted to him for his enthusiasm, devotion, and talent.

At the time of his retirement, Sam was directing the Toledo Choral Society, the Toledo Concert Band's Music Under the Stars series at the Toledo Zoo, the Perrysburg Symphony Orchestra, and music at First Congregational Church. He was also going to direct the Toledo Symphony Orchestra's program the following January entitled "An Evening in Vienna."

Following his retirement, in the summers of 1984 and 1985, Sam and his son Tom ran a program called Summer Winds. The program was sponsored through the Toledo Parks and Recreation Department and brought together 50 to 60 high school musicians from all around the area. Tom wrote the arrangements for the band. They rehearsed at the University of Toledo and played concerts in city parks throughout Toledo.

No matter what the setting, Sam was a dedicated professional educator who went the extra mile for students. Procuring a haircut for a student to assure he would not be made fun of by the others, and driving a student up to University of Michigan to help him get a scholarship there—the same kindness that had been shown to him in his youth—were not unusual events. He never stopped. He inspired students to achieve more than their talents would seem to allow. His sincerity and undying wealth of knowledge endeared him to his students. They loved and trusted him. It was a win-win situation for everyone, and many of his former students can be found both across the country and abroad, pursuing music as professional musicians and as an avocation.

Sam spent over 30 years teaching music at secondary and collegiate levels. According to many of Sam's former students, his abilities as an educator were some of his greatest gifts. He didn't teach just music,

Sam in the garden with some of his fresh vegetables. (Photo by Lloyd Ransom, courtesy *The Blade*).

according to his students, but he taught many life lessons, leaving an indelible mark on each and every pupil. Some of the recurring themes that arise when speaking to his former students was Sam's unconventional approach—he didn't follow the "old rules;" he was always striving to be current and relevant, he was amazingly creative, and he inspired the best in every student.

Chapter 6
Music Under the Stars

While Sam was a beloved educator, his love of music was also evident in his many other musical endeavors outside of a school setting. From bands to choirs, orchestras to music lessons, Sam did much to earn the moniker of Toledo's "Mr. Music." Of all of his additional responsibilities, his work with the Toledo Concert Band's Music Under the Stars (MUTS) is what endeared him to thousands in the Toledo area.

MUTS was the signature summertime cultural event in Toledo for more than half a century. The concerts were held at the Toledo Zoo amphitheater on Sunday evenings. Sam's first experience with MUTS was in 1951 when the East Toledo Youth Chorus, which he organized and directed, performed at a MUTS concert. The conductor for that concert was William Leonhardt. Just two years later, in 1953, one year after graduating from the University of Michigan, Sam would take over as music director and conductor of MUTS, beginning his almost 60-year affiliation with one of the Glass City's most cherished musical traditions.

MUTS was the brain child of Arthur Gratop, the city's Director of Public Welfare. According to an article in the August 4, 1951 issue of the *Toledo City Journal*, Gratop had previously initiated a series of Sunday evening concerts in various parks of the city, but they were not well attended. He then came up with the idea of moving the concerts to the Zoo Amphitheater. According to programs from 1950 and 1951, there were eight free concerts paid for out of the City Recreations Division

Budget and the Music and Performance Trust Fund of the Recording Industry. Ken Holland, a well-known music educator in Toledo was music director and shared conducting duties. Joseph Sainton was listed as conductor on another 1950 program. In 1952, there were ten free concerts—the first two were by the Toledo Orchestra with Wolfgang Stresseman conducting, and the final eight were by the Toledo Civic Band.

During the early years and when Sam took over in 1953, the series was arranged by the Department of Recreation, which was under the umbrella of the city's Public Welfare Department. Initially, Sam was considered an employee of the Department of Recreation. Gratop continued as Director of Public Welfare and Arthur Morse the Supervisor of Recreation. Sam spoke of these men in quite fond terms and expressed much respect for them. The commentator for the concerts at that time was Jules Blair, a widely known local radio personality and broadcaster. Blair continued in that capacity until 1959 when Joe Bisonnette, Business Manager of the Toledo Zoological Society, assumed the commentator role.

In 1953 Sam was responsible for the series but shared conducting duties with Phillip Zaugg, another Toledo music educator. Zaugg's affiliation with the series ended that summer, leaving Sam to continue with all conducting duties as well as all of the planning and organizing work for the season, which consisted of eight to ten concerts. The programs in the early and mid-1950s included lots of wonderful band music as well as weekly sing-a-longs such as "I've been Working on the Railroad," "My Country, 'Tis of Thee," and church hymns such as "Faith of Our Fathers" and "Holy, Holy, Holy." Soloists were engaged as well and included vocalists, instrumentalists, dance companies, and magicians.

Sam had some very funny stories from his early years with MUTS. One such story was when the band performed Tchaikovsky's *1812 Overture*. The percussionist at the time was a man named Heman

Sam conducting Music Under the Stars in the Toledo Zoo Amphitheater in the 1950s.

Mygatt. According to Sam, Mygatt was a well-known drummer, who was a bit crusty and always had a cigar hanging out of the corner of his mouth. During the rehearsal, when it came to the cannon shots, nothing happened. After they finished, Sam asked "What about the cannon shots?" Mygatt replied, "Don't worry sonny, they'll be there tonight." The night of the concert Mygatt had a small cannon set up at the back of the stage. As the band played, Sam cued the first cannon shot. Mygatt fired the cannon and, as Sam told it, it went off with such force that the whole band shell filled with smoke as well as all the dust and pigeon droppings it shook loose from every nook and cranny of the structure. The sound was so loud that between the debris and the noise, band members were unable to breathe or hear for at least the next dozen measures. There was even more chaos in the clarinet section as the cannon debris hit their backsides, leaving at least one musician with singed trousers.

Gratop and everyone else involved with MUTS had a particularly difficult time in 1955 when rising costs forced the city to drop its sponsorship of the popular program. MUTS was then underwritten by the Music Performance Trust Fund and interested businesses and individuals, along with some support from the zoo. The eight years from 1955 to 1963 were the most financially challenging for MUTS. The series was sponsored on a week-to-week basis with no certainty as to how many concerts there would be during any one season. Sam was regularly soliciting funds to keep the series going and it was during these years that a free will offering was also collected during the concerts to help with the costs.

In 1961 Edward Lamb, a wealthy well-known labor attorney, businessman, and broadcasting executive, stepped up and made a ten-concert season possible. This was a particularly good year. The following year, some assistance was provided by Toledo Edison and the Toledo Savings and Loan League, but it was not enough for the entire season. The News of Music column in the July 11, 1962 edition of the *Toledo*

Blade announced that MUTS would be collecting offerings at their performances.

The new pass-the-hat policy created another responsibility, in that the money had to be counted after each concert. Three people were required to be present to count the money, one of whom was Sam. One night, everyone else had gone home and the three of them were in an office on the zoo grounds counting the money when a zoo employee burst in in a panic and said, "come quick, the wallaby got out." They jumped up and all three went running out to help as Sam was yelling, "Wait a minute, what's a wallaby and how do you catch one?" Luckily, the zoo employee was able to corner the wallaby, and knew how to handle it, so the other three only had to provide moral support.

It wasn't until 1963, when Toledo Edison agreed to fund an entire season of eight concerts, that MUTS was again assured of a full season. Edison continued as the sole sponsor of MUTS for the next ten years. It was a marriage made in heaven. Sam and the band loved having a guaranteed eight concerts and the electric utility loved the MUTS programs. In a community memo Toledo Edison wrote, "None of the community services we participate in gives us greater satisfaction than sponsorship of MUTS. Samuel P. Szor and the Toledo Concert Band are doing a wonderful job. Your enthusiastic and record attendance at these concerts certainly proves it."

Sam was more than a conductor and fundraiser for MUTS. He was responsible not only for the artistic planning of the series, but also for the nuts and bolts of making it run. He hired someone to contract and manage band personnel. For a short time, it was Rodney Davis, who was manager of the Toledo Symphony at the time. Subsequently, Don Seeman, a clarinetist with the band, took over these responsibilities and handled them for almost twenty years. Sam focused his efforts on procuring sponsors to keep the series going, getting the word out about the concerts, printing of the programs every week, hiring all

Sam conducting the Toledo Concert Band in the 1960s.

guest soloists or acts, tending to any technical needs for the concerts—including finding ushers for concerts—as well as preparing the music. In 1975, the Toledo Symphony Orchestra management came on board to assist in handling these responsibilities.

Concerts were broadcast on WTOL/WCWA radio on both AM and FM stations from the late 1950s through the early 1970s. Radio broadcasts were appreciated by the listening audience but didn't do justice to some of the special guests such as Eloise and her trained elephant (who used to appear in the early 1960s), or the magicians or baton twirlers. For major undertakings such as Carl Orffs *Carmina Burana,* the radio audience could hear the chorus and instruments, but missed the accompanying ballet danced by the Kerwin Ballet Theatre. Another undertaking of note in 1967 was the performance of *Ray and the Gospel Singer,* a comic opera in three scenes written by Toledo's Elizabeth Gould with libretto by Eugene Hochman. WGTE TV solved those problems in the 1990s when they agreed to broadcast an hour of each concert. Many people who were not able to get to the zoo really missed those broadcasts when they ended.

Ray Hunter, a business manager for the zoo, took over as commentator in 1965 and continued for three years, after which Tom Bollin stepped in. Bollin, a former student of Sam's at Woodward High School and executive director of elementary education for the Toledo Public Schools at the time, was experienced in the fields of music and theater. He wrote his own script as commentator, including introductions of the music selections, and made this role his own. He became a pillar of the series, serving as commentator from 1968 to 1988.

Another one of Sam's favorite stories was about an idea for a Barge Concert in 1962. It was a Labor Day concert to be performed on a barge in the Maumee River at Walbridge Park. Inspiration for the concert came from Handel's *Water Music Suite* and *Royal Fireworks Suite* which were on the program, Handel being one of Sam's favorite composers. He persuaded a marine contracting firm to lend him the craft which was then spray painted by four of his students from Woodward. There were quite a lot of details to work out. Sam recalled how they had to find a barge big enough for the whole band, they needed electricity on the barge for the stand lights, then there were the logistics of getting the percussion instruments onto the barge and all the band members with their instruments, and so on.

Finally, it was all worked out. On the day of the concert, everyone was in place and everything was a go. The only problem was the barge had been towed so far out into the river, that the people on the riverbanks could barely hear the band when they started to play. Sam thought the water would reflect the sound, but that did not happen. Towing them in closer was not an option, so it seemed this gargantuan effort was all of for naught. Thankfully, the fireworks at the end of the concert kept the crowd happy. While in later years there were several concerts on a ship—the Willis B. Boyer—there was never another barge concert.

The concerts in the 1960s were wildly popular. At the time, the capacity of the Toledo Zoo amphitheater was listed as 4,950, and articles in local newspapers in 1963 routinely documented crowds of 4,000 to 5,000 at MUTS performances. According to the *Toledo Blade*, the opening concert of the 1964 season drew a record setting crowd of 6,000, creating a standing room only situation. A rain-out of the second concert in 1964 resulted in more than 500 calls to the zoo asking when the concert would be held.

The Dana Corporation and The Andersons joined as sponsors in the 1970s, providing continuing financial stability for MUTS and ensuring a full series of eight concerts each summer. The two sponsors presented Sam with a silver tray in 1977 to acknowledge Sam's efforts over the years. The engraving read:

To Samuel P. Szor
In grateful recognition and with sincere appreciation for 25 years of service to the community as Musical Director and Conductor of the Music Under the Stars concert series.
"Play it again Sam"

Some of concerts in the 1970s were especially fulfilling for Sam, as both of his sons were playing in the band—Terry on trumpet and Tom on keyboard. Tom's arrangements of top twenty hits were played as encores. Starting with "You're the One That I Want" from *Grease* in 1978, he continued writing ovation worthy encores through the 1980s,

1990s, and into the 2000s. Songs by Huey Lewis and the News and other such artists were popular in the 1980s. Some favorite tunes over the years included the "Macarena," "YMCA," "Achy Breaky Heart," and "Pirates of the Caribbean."

Sam's commitment to his work was undeniable. An excerpt from a 1976 MUTS program states: "'Great music starts with the people, the masses' is a philosophy that influences much of Samuel P. Szor's programming for MUTS. 'We have no rules. I'll program Broadway, pop, rock, gospel, anything, if I can see in my mind a way to make it interesting and stirring to our audiences.'"

In 1978, Sam's 25th year as program director and conductor of MUTS, his bio in the concert programs that year recalled everything he had done with the organization to that point:

> Samuel P. Szor has "worn many hats" to bring MUTS audiences interesting programming. He has raised the baton on band, orchestra, chorus, ballet, opera, musical theatre, and oratorio, and some of the highlights of the past quarter century have included ballet: Aaron Copland's *Billy the Kid*, Hershy Kay's *Stars and Stripes Forever* and Robert Prince's *Opus Jazz*. (all danced by the Kerwin Theater Ballet) Oratorio: Duruflé's *Requiem*, Haydn's *Mass in the Time of War* and the Brahms *Liebeslieder Waltzes*. Opera: Menotti's *The Telephone*. Musical theatre: Bernstein's *Trouble in Tahiti* and of course, band music—all the splendid marches of John Philip Sousa. Sam took over the musical direction and conducting of MUTS in 1953. It was just in the formulative stages at that point and he has led it down the path to the success it is today."

Innovative programming, always a hallmark of Sam's concerts, was part of the success of MUTS for so many years. Another part was his careful preparation, as evidenced by his heavily marked musical scores. Every measure was analyzed harmonically. He used red and blue pencils to mark, for instance, a juicy chord—it would be circled in red with a notation of "WOW!"—or it might be a cymbal crash here or the bass line there, things that had to come out to make the music come alive, to get the sound he wanted, to make the music "come off the page" as he would say. Then there was his presence, that special energy he brought to every performance created such a wonderful connection with the audience, for after all, it was always all about the audience. His enthusiasm and talent made for wonderful musical experiences enjoyed by thousands at the zoo and other venues as well.

Hundreds of musicians have played in the band over the years. It

Sam conducting the Toledo Concert Band on the *Willis B. Boyer* (Photo by Herral Long, courtesy *The Blade*).

is known the world over not as the Music Under the Stars band or the Toledo Concert Band, but simply as the "Zoo Band." The band typically had one two-and-a-half-hour rehearsal to prepare for each concert, and it is a testament to the talent and skill of the musicians that they could put on such challenging programs so successfully.

The band also played concerts at Lakeside, Ohio for many years, and at the Rose Garden Arts Festival that used to be held behind the Safety Building in downtown Toledo. During the 1990s for the Fourth of July they would play on the grounds of the Hayes Presidential Center in Fremont, Ohio during the afternoon, and then head back to Toledo to perform downtown just before the evening's fireworks display. The band also performed an annual concert in Van Wert, Ohio from the 1990s into the early 2000s. There were also concerts, usually two a season, at Maumee Bay State Park throughout most of the 1990s.

Concerts on the Willis B. Boyer, a retired great lakes freighter that was anchored in downtown Toledo, occurred with some regularity and were quite popular. The band also played a couple of times for festivals in Monroe, Michigan, and at the Fulton County Fairgrounds. They played for the opening of Dillards in the Franklin Park Mall, for an Ohio Music Education Association state conference, and for the dedication of St. Anne's Hospital.

In addition to the zoo band, MUTS would also feature other musicians who were eager to perform at one of the summer's hottest gigs. Calls would begin soon after the first of every new year from individuals and groups hoping to perform at MUTS. Some sent tapes or CDs or Sam would go to see or hear a person or group before he made his decision. It was a wonderful venue for showcasing talent.

Some of the most memorable individual performers include Bob McGrath, a decades-long star on Sesame Street and one of Sam's fraternity brothers. He performed at MUTS in 1954 and again in 1975. Shirley Verrett Carter, Mezzo-soprano later turned soprano, soloed at

MUTS in the 1950s before she went on to a stellar career with the New York City Opera, opera houses in Europe, and the Metropolitan Opera. It was at MUTS around 1989 that tenor Shawn Mathey made his public debut singing with his father, the incredibly talented tenor, Richard Mathey. It was a magical moment. Shawn went on to become an in-demand tenor across the United States and in European opera houses. A popular and perhaps the most frequent soloist at MUTS was soprano Judith Hauman Dye.

In addition to many vocal soloists, there were also appearances by a variety of other groups and musicians. Some of those included the Westgate Dinner Theater cast, the popular group from the 1970s called The Villagers, and the Ritz, a national and international award-winning barbershop quartet. There were also many dance groups, including the Kerwin and Cassandra ballet companies as well as the Ballet Theatre of Toledo. Wonderful instrumentalists were featured guests too, such as Lynn Klock saxophonist, Lowell Greer on french horn, John Mohler on clarinet, Ric Wolkins on trumpet, and the group Sax 4th Avenue. The Blue Grass fiddlers wowed the crowd too—the DePue boys followed by Seth Gangwer.

Guest performers have fond memories of their performances at MUTS.

> *Sam was fond of turning a handshake into a kiss of the back of the hand…except he would turn that into kissing the back of his own hand! I always got a warm laugh out of that clever joke.*
>
> *Sam used to call some of the musicians in the Toledo Concert Band after the performances to get a feel for what people thought. He was deeply concerned about reaching audiences and about people enjoying the concerts. I've never known anyone so outwardly dedicated to reaching, satisfying, and entertaining the audience as Sam.*
>
> *Sam was committed to producing a Variety Show—a formula common in theaters during the early twentieth century, and later on television. But this was a variety show with a Concert Band as the centerpiece and the outdoors as the theatre, and he sustained and*

transported that successful formula into the twenty-first century. It was a unique Toledo treasure of which I was deeply proud to have been a small player.

Shannon Ford
saxophonist, member of Sax 4th Avenue

While MUTS was a staple of the summer music scene in Northwest Ohio, one cannot forget its venue was one of the country's leading zoos, and every once and a while some of the residents would work their way into a performance. In the 1970s Dan Danford used to come out in a "Talk to the Animals" segment during the concert. He would bring out an animal to present to the audience and do some introduction and explaining about the animal, where it was from, etc. On one occasion, Danford came out with a ten- to twelve-foot boa constrictor and promptly put it around Sam's neck as he proceeded to talk about the snake. Sam froze. He had no idea that was going to happen and could only say after that he was glad the audience was far enough away that they could not see the look of sheer terror on his face or the cold sweat running down his back. "Only my launderer knew how terrified I really was," he mused.

Animals used to be in close proximity to the amphitheater, and sometimes, when the wind came from a certain direction, the evening air could be quite aromatic. One of Tom Szor's early childhood memories is of a bear kept in a cage just off to the side of the amphitheater—apparently it was part of an animal act that occurred each day at the zoo—and the bear would beat its chains in rhythm with the music during the concert. John Ginther, who played in the band for many decades, related a time when the featured soloist played the euphonium. When he started to play, something about the sound really riled one of the lions who started to roar and roar—and just wouldn't stop. The audience began to laugh and eventually the soloist and band too. Everyone had to take a break to regain their composure so they could carry on. It also was not unusual for the peacocks to chime in, too, especially when a soprano was singing.

Sam Szor gave me my first solo performance opportunity in Toledo, for which I am forever grateful. He was director of the Toledo Choral Society, which gave an annual performance of Handel's "Messiah." I was new to Toledo and eager to become a part of Toledo's music world. My husband's aunt and uncle, who knew Sam from his teaching at Woodward High School, suggested I audition for him. I did, and I sang the soprano solos in that year's "Messiah," the first of many I had the pleasure of performing with Sam and his choral society. Sam opened the door for me to enter the music scene, and I then performed frequently with the Toledo Symphony, the Toledo Opera, and was a "regular" on Music Under the Stars summer concert series, of which Sam was the maestro for many years.

Working with Sam was always fun. He was a serious musician, but shared his delight in making music, especially in rehearsals, where jokes, teasing, and laughter were his inimitable style. As the paid soprano soloist in the church choir Sam directed, I appreciated Sam's careful choosing of choral music of the highest quality, which also suited the ability of the choir members, so that the music was inspiring and satisfying.

Sam had the talent for knowing each member of his orchestras and choirs and made each one feel special to be a part of the music making.

Rehearsals for "Music Under the Stars" were amazing. Normally there was only one rehearsal, usually on the stage of the Amphitheater of the Toledo Zoo, where the concerts were held, and just a few hours before the performance was to begin. There was often chaos, with sound people checking microphones, TV people checking cameras, stage hands milling about. All the while Sam kept his cool, rehearsing the musicians, making certain all was in order, and then out of the chaos, conducting a wonderful performance. Sam knew how to program music that was appealing to his audiences at these Sunday night open air concerts, giving them both classical and popular music, always of the highest standard, and the audiences loved him. He brought them into his fun of making music.

We had some interesting experiences at these outdoor concerts, such as causing the peacocks to screech when I sang high notes; having a trained bear pacing in his cage, banging his chains in a rhythm that did not match the rhythm of the piece we were performing, and then the infamous night when a pigeon lodged in the proscenium of the stage did his "business" on me just as I finished my performance. Sam stepped off the podium, came over to me, put his head on my shoulder, his body shaking with laughter. The audience thought he was overcome with emotion at my beautiful singing, but when the orchestra began to laugh, the audience realized what had happened, and began to laugh too. Soon the entire amphitheater was rocking with laughter. Sam escorted me off the stage-the first and last time I was ever "laughed" off the stage! Sam gave me many memories, from the sublime to the ridiculous! I think we both treasured that one in particular.

Sam Szor was truly "Mr. Music" of Toledo.

Judy Hauman Dye
frequent MUTS soprano soloist

The 1980s brought consistently large crowds for MUTS concerts. The opening concert of the 1981 MUTS season drew a record crowd of over 7,000. According to an article in the July 11 edition of *The Blade*, 30 minutes before the concert's scheduled 8 p.m. start time, there was a wait of twenty minutes to get into the zoo's parking lots. Latecomers found the lots full so began parking wherever they could find a space. It was standing room only inside and outside of the amphitheater. Likewise, for the finale of the 1985 season, *The Blade* reported an overflow crowd that was undeterred by the day's cloudy skies. Toledoans' fondness for MUTS can be summarized in this note received by Sam after a concert in 1999:

Dear Mr. Szor,

We took a neighbor to your last concert last night who had never in her 60-some years attended Music Under the Stars. She was simply delighted (as we always are). Thank you, and Tom, and all the members for another year of musical enjoyment and bolstering for the Toledo winter ahead! (Just like a musical multivitamin!)

Sincerely,
Dee Kirk

Gordon Ward took over the reins as commentator in 1988 and

Gordon Ward, a long-time emcee of Music Under the Stars, in a balloon crown made for him by a clown during a circus-themed MUTS.

served longer than anyone else in that role. He had an exceptional voice and did a wonderful job. He and Sam were a great team. The evening in 1992 when he emceed Sam's MUTS 40th anniversary tribute concert was great fun. He handled the evening and special events so well, and they were unique. That's the night Sam got to conduct the largest percussion section ever—a trio of elephants. After their musical performance, one of the elephants painted a picture of Sam. Gordon also emceed the 2002 celebration of Sam's 50 years in music in Toledo. The band wore "Sam gets the gold" t-shirts and lined up across the front of the stage to pass a gold baton from person to person before finally giving it to Sam. The plaque presented to him by the zoo that evening is mounted on the outside of the back wall of the amphitheater.

Sing-a-longs came and went over the years. When they were on the program, old standards were still included, but other selections had shifted to more current tunes of the day such as "Rain Drops Keep Fallin' on My Head" and "Blowin' in the Wind" in the 1970s and "You Light up My Life," "Elvira," and "Tie a Yellow Ribbon" in the 1980s.

Because Sam was responsible for the artistic decisions for the concerts, he constantly worked to keep abreast of what was happening in music in all genres: the new Broadway shows, new popular movies, pop groups, even country western. He took his responsibility to bring new exciting programs to the audiences very seriously. For many years it was tradition for the season finale to be Tchaikovsky's *1812 Overture* and Sousa's granddaddy of them all, "The Stars and Stripes Forever," with fireworks. That combination was a real crowd pleaser but ended in the late 1980s when an audience member experienced a burn in his clothes from an ember, prompting the fire marshal to call a halt to the practice.

In addition to Sam's artistic role and business management responsibilities for MUTS, he also played a big role in maintaining the zoo amphitheater for many years. Before the season opener each year, Sam would recruit family and friends to help ensure the amphitheater was ready for the summer crowds. The crew swept up all the dust, debris, and pigeon droppings before breaking out the hoses to wash everything down. Sometimes risers had to be moved back into place or repaired. After everything was cleaned, any holes in the walls and doors would be patched. Then the painting began. Sam actually had an account at Sherwin-Williams just for MUTS. The walls were painted as far as could be reached with long poles and rollers, with volunteers trying to keep it even all the way around; one year when it was looking particularly grubby, they managed to paint the entire back wall with the assistance of just a ladder. The risers also got a fresh coat of paint, with the fronts of the risers getting a different design each year. The backstage area and bathrooms were also cleaned, and burned out light bulbs in the shell were replaced, as far up as could be reached. The team of volunteers were thrilled one year when Toledo Edison sent out one of their big boom trucks and replaced all the bulbs on the stage. It was such a blessing.

By West, left, and Sam, performing at the celebration of Sam's 35th year as conductor of Music Under the Stars.

Of course, Sam paid just as much attention to his appearance for the concerts. Even on the hottest of nights, he wore his formal attire. Russell's Tuxedo Shop fixed up Sam every week, often with a vest that had something to do with the theme of the upcoming concert. Two shirts were included so he could put on a dry one at intermission. Gordon Ward used to bring an electrolyte drink to share so the pair could stay hydrated.

No one worked harder at promoting MUTS than Sam. He was not a morning person, but there were days he would be up having coffee by 5 a.m. so he could be alert and ready for a 6 a.m. radio spot or TV interview. He knew almost from memory the phone numbers of *The Blade* and the local TV and radio stations, and called them frequently. He might say to *The Blade*, "Hey, it'll be a great photo-op at the concert this Sunday. Send out one of your photographers. We'll have 5,000 American flags waving."

Sam was very appreciative of the sponsors of the series, but he knew he could not expect the money to continue to come in if the crowds were not good. He worked tirelessly to ensure success. His commitment to the program was unwavering. In his 60 years at the helm of MUTS, he missed only one concert—the first concert of the 2007 season—when he was just out of the hospital for a serious medical event.

Toledo Edison/First Energy and Dana continued to be dedicated sponsors during the 1980s and 1990s as well as the Andersons in the 1980s and picking up again in the 2000s. In 1993, when two corporate sponsors pulled out due to economic reasons, the number of concerts for that year fell into question. Eventually new corporate sponsors stepped forward for that year, but henceforth, securing sponsors became an annual challenge. An eight-concert season continued until 2009, when only six concerts were held. Scarcity of funding and health issues for Sam combined to decrease concert numbers to four in 2010 and zero in 2011. In 2012, Sam's 60th year of MUTS, there were six concerts

Judy and Sam in costume for the 1987 Constitution Day Celebration in Flint, Michigan. Sam, dressed as John Philip Sousa, was guest conductor of the Flint Concert Band, and Judy was the featured soprano soloist.

with guest conductors and Sam conducting one or two pieces on each program.

In addition to the Toledo Concert "Zoo" Band, Sam had the opportunity to do some guest conducting as well. The most memorable for him was the famous Goldman Band of New York City, founded by Edwin Franko Goldman, one of the most significant American band composers of the early twentieth century and founder of the band. In 1989 Sam received the call inviting him to conduct this most prestigious band, and in mid-July he traveled to New York City to prepare for and conduct three concerts with the Goldman band. The first was a July 21 concert at noon in Central Park in Manhattan, then on July 22 a 3 p.m. concert in Prospect Park and an 8 p.m. concert in Seaside Park, both in the borough of Brooklyn.

He was also guest conductor of the Flint, Michigan Concert Band for their September 17, 1987 Constitution Day Celebration. Sam dressed as John Philip Sousa for this concert and his wife, Judy, was the featured soprano soloist.

Chapter 7
Orchestras

Sam's association with area orchestras began with the Toledo Symphony Orchestra (TSO) in 1954, when he joined the orchestra as the second bassoon player for the 1954-55 season. He continued as second bassoon with TSO on a regular basis through the 1963-64 season and played occasionally after that. During this period he also played with the Toledo Opera Orchestra for about nine years.

When he stopped playing his instruments in the 1960s, Sam turned his focus to conducting. His interest in conducting didn't start at the University of Michigan—in fact he tested out of his conducting course because he wasn't learning from it—but rather from watching the opera conductors that came through Toledo. He talked about everything they had to focus on—not only the score, but the stage, the singers, making music, and keeping the show moving. He gleaned as much as he could from their rehearsal and conducting techniques. Sam was criticized at times for his somewhat unconventional movement when conducting, but it was from the opera conductors that he learned to use his whole body to get the job done.

I had the great honor of working with Sam starting in 1985 when I joined the Toledo Symphony. I played under his directorship in the Music Under the Stars and Toledo Symphony concerts.
Sam Szor was quite a character! He was certainly one of the friendliest people I have ever met and made friends right away with everyone. He had a keen sense of humor, and a personality larger than

Sam playing the bassoon with the Toledo Symphony Orchestra.

life, yet was also very passionate about music and devoted his career to bringing fine music to Toledo.

With Sam it was all about the joy of making music. Whether it was patriot music, show tunes or the "Messiah," Sam's appreciation and deep love of the music was conveyed. I remember so many times being moved and was sometimes even choked up by the words in anything from show tunes to the "Messiah" just by watching how they impacted him.

Rehearsals were always a happy occasion for Sam, even if we had a lot of work to get done. Sam would almost always walk over to me while I was getting my instrument out. I knew by his approaching smile that he had a good joke or a great story for me. I would also get updates on the Hungarian dishes he recently made and the status of his incredible vegetable garden. He would also ask how everything was going with me since we last saw each other. He considered his colleagues his friends. We all benefited too from Sam's lightheartedness and great sense of humor. Often mid piece during the rehearsal Sam would have to share something to make us laugh. We would grin and put our instruments down whenever he would start with, "I just have to tell you something..."

Sam so loved people—all his friends, his audience and his colleagues—and was so happy to have the opportunity to work with others to create great music together. He advanced music in the Toledo area and brought joy to so many people throughout his life. He respected and appreciated the musicians he worked with so much, and we so respected and appreciated him! I am so thankful to have had all those years to work with Sam. He certainly was one of a kind and is genuinely irreplaceable!

Kim Bryden Loch
first chair oboe, Toledo Symphony Orchestra

Sam had been conducting the concert band at Music Under the Stars since 1953, and in 1979 made his official conducting debut with the Toledo Symphony Orchestra when they engaged him to conduct one of their Pops concerts. It was a concert for Mother's Day featuring 17-year-old pianist, Hyun Suk Choi as soloist. A photo of Choi with her mother and Sam with his mother in front of the Museum graced the first page of the second section of May 12, 1979 edition of *The Blade*, to remind people of the concert on the following day.

Boris Nelson, *The Blade's* music critic, gave the classical part of the program a very good review. He didn't care much for the contemporary pops music—such as John Williams *Star Wars* and Charlie Smalls *The Wiz*—but he concluded his review noting:

> The audience loved it and rewarded the conductor and orchestra with waves of applause, and the encore, a sort of Szor signature, John Philip Sousa's 'The Stars and Stripes Forever,' was not only mild in comparison (to the contemporary scores) but genuine music without having to resort to assaulting the ears. The rhythmic clapping by the audience showed just how much people miss this sort of music, which was greeted with a very spontaneous standing ovation—for Maestro Sousa and Mr. Szor and the orchestra…

From 1979 through 2003 Sam continued to conduct a variety of concerts with the TSO. For a number of years the symphony sponsored "An Evening in Vienna" at the Masonic Theatre on New Year's Eve. Yuval Zaliouk, then conductor of the TSO, conducted the concert portion and Sam conducted the orchestra for the Viennese Ball that followed in the theatre's Great Hall. In September of 1984, he was called on to fill in for a Classics concert for Zaliouk who was in Israel attending the funeral of his father. The concert was titled "A Carnival of Bach." He also led the orchestra during the ground-breaking ceremony for the Owens-Illinois building at One Seagate in 1979 and led a group for the symphony called the Amazing Classical Band in the early 1980s. In the late 1980s Sam conducted the TSO for the Razzle Dazzle New Year's Eve parties that were held downtown. The TSO played in the Grand Ballrooms of the Hotel Sofitel and the Toledo Marriott Portside Hotel.

In 1991, Sam began the Casual Concert Series with the TSO, a series of four concerts a year in a format similar to Music Under the Stars, promoted as "Hear More Szor!" Some jokingly called them "Music Under the Ceiling." The series was held at the Masonic (Stranahan)

Theatre, which seats about 2,500 people. The concerts were popular and very well attended. Sam usually conducted three of the four concerts with the primary and resident conductors taking one or two per season. In time, the Halloween Spooktacular became part of that series with other conductors also taking part. The series continued through 2002-03. The Halloween concert continued annually with Sam participating through 2005.

Sam's conducting with the TSO continued in the 1990s and included:

Guest Conductor on the 50th Anniversary Concert at the Toledo Zoo Amphitheater in 1993;

Conductor of a concert to open the holiday season with a Boston Pops-style concert at Seagate Center;

Conductor of "A Musical Valentine" February 12, 1993 held at Gesu Catholic Church;

Conductor in a special appearance of TSO at Maumee Bay State Park around Memorial Day in 1994;

Conductor at Put-in-Bay in 1993-94 and 1994-95 seasons;

Conductor for Young People's fourth grade concerts from 1991 to 2002;

Conductor for concerts at the Ritz Theater in Tiffin, Ohio in 1992-93 and 1993-94 seasons;

Conductor for New Year's Eve Special at Trinity Episcopal Church in 1993;

Conductor for program in the Tecumseh Civic Auditorium, Tecumseh, Michigan in 1993-94 season;

Conductor for multiple holiday programs at St. Patrick's of Heatherdowns Catholic church in the 1993-1996;

> Conductor for concerts at Sacred Heart Catholic
> Church and St. Stephen's Catholic Church in
> 1997-98 series;

> Conductor for a "Riverfront Performance" in the
> 1996/97 season;

> Conductor for a concert in St. Thomas Aquinas
> Catholic Church in the 1998-99 season; and

> Conductor with Flash Cadillac (an American retro
> rock 'n' roll band) in concert twice—once at the
> zoo (1995-96) and later at the Stranahan Theater

After the Casual Concerts ended in 2002-03, Sam continued to participate in the Halloween concert for a couple of years more, but as the Symphony resident conductor took over much of what Sam had done in the past, his association with the TSO continued primarily through their connection of management of Music Under the Stars. Keith McWatters, the manager of the TSO, is the person with whom Sam had the most contact over the years for both MUTS and TSO concerts.

Sam was a great musician, and a terrific conductor. But above all, he was an entertainer. So, Sam was referred to as "Mr. Music" ... Not "Mr. Conductor" ... not "Maestro" (though sometimes those were used) He was MR. MUSIC! And I always assumed it was because, with Sam ... it was indeed, all about the music. It didn't matter if it was a Bach Cantata or a Sousa March ... all music was important, deserved to be listened to ... and if it was music ... it should be entertaining and enjoyed.

When it was appropriate, the delivery was often as important as the music itself. So Sam spent a lot of his limitless energy preparing concerts to be a whole experience ... not just an opportunity to hear some music, but the opportunity to "see" and experience a concert. It was the overall experience that was important

And he was such a good sport in delivering a performance. Whether he was asked to serenade an elephant that was painting, wear a live snake around his neck, or dress as (a darn good) John Philip Sousa ... he delivered an experience! But above all ... the music was good.

An important point with Mr. Music: It was all about the audience … always. And a close second … the musicians. At the end of every show … Sam would always ask …"do you think they liked it" referring to the audience. That was what every performance was about: pleasing the audience. Once we determined that the audience enjoyed the show, it was on to the band (or orchestra). "Do you think 'the guys' liked it" (Sam always referred to all of the musicians as "the guys.") It was ever so important to Sam that folks enjoyed themselves. That was his goal, above all else.

Sam Szor was the consummate professional. Always early … not just on time. Always prepared…for everything and anything! Always working the crowd or chatting it up with the band. Simply doing the right thing. Sam was always 'on'. He invented the 'git 'er dun' attitude!

Performing was always fun with Sam. He had fun … we all had fun! His energy and joy in the music was contagious.

I always felt that I was blessed to enjoy a special camaraderie with Sam. Others probably felt this way as well, Sam was good at that. But Sam and I worked a lot behind the scenes prior to, and worked closely (musically) during the performance. I often felt (as his drummer for 30 plus years) that we worked in tandem to create a force of rhythm or a simple energy within the music. So when a performance was over, there was always a wink and nod from across the stage. We never showered each other with praise, just a nod to say "good job … they dug it!" That was enough.

Sometimes the winks happened during a piece, during a concert. Something would happen, or I'd play a certain something…and our eyes would meet and a spontaneous laugh would happen. Brief as they were, those moments were so much fun!

There was a place in 'Selections from the Sound of Music' where I would place a cymbal crash…and Sam would always glance at me, twinkle in his eye, every time it happened. I was never sure why … but our shoulders would go and we'd enjoy a brief giggle in the middle of a concert. Fun times…no better way to make a living!

As Mr. Music, Sam was gracious and humble, demanding yet forgiving, outgoing and boisterous … yet reverent and respectful. I miss him.

Keith McWatters
manager, the Toledo Symphony Orchestra

Sam loved his work with bands, but he also had an affinity for orchestral music. He wanted to learn more orchestral repertoire, study the scores, and conduct more orchestral works. So, when presented with the opportunity in 1970, he took over as the music director and conductor for the Perrysburg Symphony Orchestra (PSO).

The idea for the PSO can be traced back to Judy Beck, who, in 1959, dusted off her bass to play in the pit orchestra for a Suburban Singer's production. The Singers was a choral group based in Perrysburg. She enjoyed it so much she wanted to continue to play and began calling parents of band students to see if there was any interest. Frank Menichetti, a music teacher and band director at Perrysburg High School, agreed to serve as the group's conductor if there were ten interested people—there were 25 at the first meeting. The Perrysburg Symphony Orchestra was subsequently founded in 1961. The group has continued ever since, and consistently counts around 50 to 60 members. There were two directors before Sam: Menichetti and Joe Morin. Morin was a music teacher for Maumee City Schools, directed the school's orchestra, and played violin in the Toledo Symphony Orchestra.

The PSO has always been a diverse group of people. They have had doctors, truck drivers, teachers, people in their 80s to those just out of high school and everyone in between. In the early years, 98 percent were from Perrysburg, but that decreased over time. According to an article in the October 28, 1986 edition of the Bowling Green *Sentinel-Tribune*, members were coming from as far away as Archbold and Fremont, Ohio, and Bedford, Michigan.

Rehearsals were held every Tuesday evening from 8 to 10 p.m. at Perrysburg High School. When Sam took over in August he had to get to work to prepare for a concert scheduled November 22. In an article in the August 27, 1970 edition of the *Fremont News-Messenger* announcing Sam's appointment, he put out a call for additional string, woodwind, brass, and percussion players. For his first concert, the PSO included six first violins, eight second violins, four violas, two cellos, four string basses, one harp, two percussion, three flutes, two oboes and English horns, three clarinets, three bassoons, five trumpets, five French horns, three trombones, and one tuba. The program consisted of works by Jules Massenet, Johann Sebastian Bach, Samuel Barber, Richard Strauss, Benjamin Britten, and the *Mass in G Major* by Franz Schubert with the Perrysburg Symphony Arts Chorus. Traditionally the orchestra performed two classical and one pops concert each season.

Over the years under Sam's leadership, the orchestra improved steadily. The impossible became a reality through continual upgrading and years of what Sam described as "good personnel getting better." The article in the October 28, 1986 edition of the Bowling Green *Sentinel-Tribune*, described Sam's approach to the PSO:

> Just because the performers aren't all professionals doesn't mean that their director doesn't expect great music from them. Though Szor explained he isn't "hard-nosed" about his music, he does take it very seriously. "I really care and want to make it good," he said.
>
> He doesn't just let the symphony members skip over difficult areas, but instead drills them through it until the rough spots are smoothed out. To Szor the greatest joy in music is listening to the improvements made from when a piece is first played to when it is practiced to perfection.
>
> According to Szor ... the sense of achievement after perfecting a piece of music is often greater when working with non-professionals. "There's a really good feeling, like "hey, we did it," he explained.

According to the Perrysburg Symphony Orchestra's website, during Sam's twenty years at the helm "he brought a higher level of sophistication to the orchestra program. The concerts had central themes and often featured soloists and ensembles. Szor's contributions were innovative and included the Community Messiah Sing-Along and the Valentines Dinner Concert."

While most of the orchestra's classical concerts were played in the

Perrysburg High School auditorium and the gymnasium for the pops concerts, other venues included St. Rose Catholic Church, St. Stephen's Catholic Church, St. Hedwig Cultural Center, First Congregational Church, and St. Patrick Historic Church.

Sam used to tell the story about a concert at St. Rose Catholic Church. There was a "big fella" who had helped with moving the instruments and setting up for the concert in the church. During the concert while the orchestra was playing Handel's "Water Music," the man sat on a sink that was attached to the wall in the sacristy. Under his weight the sink broke loose from the wall and water was squirting all over. Sam used to say, "While we were playing the *Water Music*, we could hear the water spraying in the back room. We really brought the Water Music to life!"

On the occasion of the 25th anniversary year of the PSO, the November 24, 1985 fall concert was reviewed by Blade music critic Boris Nelson. The program consisted of Rossini's "Overture" *Barber of Seville*, "Vivace" from *Piano Concert No. 1 in F-sharp minor* by Rachmaninoff, *Prelude in C, Op. 12, No. 7* by Prokofieff, "Scherzo" from *Sonata No. 18 in E-flat, Op. 31, No. 3* by Beethoven all with Anthony Pattin on piano, and Schumann's *Symphony No. 1 in B-flat, Op. 38*. Of the performance, Nelson wrote:

> Not all orchestras equal the Boston or Cleveland orchestras but they exist nevertheless for the sheer joy of making music in an ensemble and growing in musical wisdom. Such an organization is the Perrysburg Symphony Orchestra, an ensemble of some 50 instrumentalists, which last Sunday afternoon opened its 25th season with its fall concert at the Perrysburg High School auditorium.
>
> The orchestra suffers apparently no generation gap, since its members range in age from somewhere around 18 to 80, and consists frankly and proudly of a good mixture of amateurs in the original sense the word: those who engage in an activity for the sheer love of it. Under the direction of Samuel P. Szor, they

rehearse regularly and tackle music which at times stretches their technical agility, but no matter - they "dig" what they are doing and surprisingly or not they often do quite well by it.

Take for example, the opening Overture to "The Barber of Seville," which they played with elan and accuracy. The Robert Schumann "Spring Symphony" his first, was managed well enough until the final movement, when things went into some heavy sledding, and understandably so. It is not an easy work but a beautiful one, and that was probably the reason both conductor and orchestra were attracted to it. But in the previous movements there was a pleasant string tone and accuracy.

The accompaniment of a piano concerto takes an extraordinary sense of musicianship in just about every case, and Rachmaninoff's lesser-played first concerto is certainly no exception. Toledo pianist Anthony Pattin was the soloist in the Vivace and played it with aplomb and a nice feeling for the characteristics of the composer's not yet fully developed style. And the orchestra managed. It was in the subsequent two piano works that Mr. Pattin showed his consistent growth as a musician-pianist. Never a mere mechanic, he used his fine technique to poetize the Prokofieff Prelude and to give the proper joy and lightness to Beethoven's Scherzo. He infused each with spirit, and the audience appreciated his efforts.

Twenty-five years is a long time and a proud time for such an orchestra as the Perrysburg and its efforts are not in vain, nor are they exclusively for themselves. Musicians, professionals and amateurs alike, need to perform the music that interests them, and that means that together they deserve community support and an audience.

In addition to their three-concert season, they also participated in community events such as the Diamond Jubilee Celebration of St. Stephen's Church in 1973, a joint concert with the Toledo Choral Society in 1976 to perform Bach's *Magnificat*, and a Christmas concert with the Woodville Community Chorus in 1973.

The Valentine's Day concerts were held in the Perrysburg Holiday

Inn French Quarter. The first one was perhaps the most challenging because of an ice storm that evening. Many of the orchestra members arrived late and some not at all. Sam was invited back in February 2001 to conduct the Orchestra's Gala Valentine's Day Dinner Concert which was held at Owens Community College.

In 1986 the orchestra had a large string section with about 26 violins, four violas, seven cellos, and three basses. The continual upgrade and years of good personnel getting better allowed Sam to program more challenging music as the years went on. Some of the Symphonies performed by the Perrysburg orchestra during Sam's tenure included:

1983 Schubert, *Symphony Now 9 in C*
1985 Mendelssohn, *Symphony No. 4 in A Major*
1985 Schumann, *Symphony No. 1 in B Flat*
1986 Dvorak, *Symphony No. 8 in G major*
1988 Sibelius, *Symphony No. 2 in D Major*
1989 Brahms, *Symphony No. 3 in F*
1989 Haydn, *Symphony No. 100 "Militaire"*
1990 Beethoven, *Symphony No. 7 in A Major*
1990 Haydn, *Symphony No. 101, "The Clock"*

In addition to the symphonies, Sam brought in excellent soloists to perform concertos with the orchestra. Some of those soloists along with the concertos they performed include:

1972 Paul Schoenfield   Beethoven, *Piano Concerto No. 3*
1973 Frances Renzi   Beethoven, Piano Concerto No. 4
1978 Elaine Moore   Liszt Piano, *Concerto No. 1 in E Flat Major*
1979 Elaine Moore   Beethoven, *Piano Concerto No 3 in C minor*
1987 Elaine Moore   Rachmaninoff, *Piano Concerto No. 2*
1978 Anthony Pattin   Mendelssohn-Bartholdy, *Piano Concert No. 1*

1985	Anthony Pattin	Rachmaninoff, *Piano Concert No. 1 in F sharp minor*
1985	Tom Szor	Bach, *Piano Concerto No. 5 in F minor*
1990	Tom Szor	Handel, *Concerto in B Flat for Organ and Orchestra*
1987	Roger Jamini	Mozart, *Violin concerto No. 5*
1988	Kimberly Bryden	Vivaldi, *Concerto in F for Oboe*
1988	Michael H. Boyd	Prokofiev, *Piano Concerto No. 1, Opus 10*
1989	Ann Pope	Beethoven, *Piano concerto No. 3 in C minor, Op. 37*

Some said Sam transformed the PSO from a catch-as-catch-can organization to an on-going organization for people who enjoy performing music and performing it professionally.

Perrysburg Orchestra was one of many musical "troupes" fortunate to play under Sam's baton and inspiration. He was a consummate musician. His musical knowledge and curiosity covered all music styles, and those interests were generously shared and conveyed in a way to help players raise their levels of playing. Besides calling upon such areas as orchestral, choral, band, jazz, certainly contemporary, etc. there was, of course, his expertise in orchestral bassoon and jazz tenor saxophone that entered in. He could weave in some innuendo of information that could enable a player to find his/her voice and important line within the ensemble. And lastly, something worthy of mention was his humor. He was very quick wit and had a sense of humor that helped to keep everyone engaged.

Clark Barnes
member and past-president, Perrysburg Symphony Orchestra

Joe Meyers, a music educator in the Sylvania schools and a violist who also played with the Toledo Symphony Orchestra would sit in with the PSO for concerts when Joe Morin was conductor. He continued to play when Sam took the reins.

When Sam took over, the whole performance level of the orchestra raised with better music and more practice time. It was clear that I couldn't just drop in at the last minute anymore. The level of personnel improved and we did music that community orchestras usually can't do. His rehearsal technique was unique, often starting at the back of the piece. One of the things I learned from him and I continue to use even now, is that it's easier to analyze the whole piece before I start to work on my part. Sam's scores were always all analyzed and marked everywhere. Knowing Sam was always a good thing; we got to play good music in interesting places and it was fun. I've never known anybody who was more of a force of nature than Sam—you could count on him— whatever he said would happen would always happen.

Joe Meyers
violist, Toledo and Perrysburg Symphony Orchestras

Chapter 8
Choral Conducting

Sam's experience with choral conducting began when his high school music teacher, Cecile Vashaw, assigned him to work with the Waite High School Girls Chorus occasionally in her absence. It continued during his college years with his fraternity chorus and the East Toledo Youth Chorus, which Sam founded and conducted each summer when he was home from school. His first professional job in choral conducting came when he was hired by the Toledo Choral Society (TCS) to take over as their Music Director and Conductor in 1958. In addition to a pair of summer concerts planned for the Zoo amphitheater that year, TCS was also slated to perform Haydn's *Creation* in Lakeside, Ohio. It was the first of many years that TCS participated in the Lakeside summer concert series. Mary Clark Anderson was the accompanist for TCS at the time.

TCS is the longest continuously performing musical organization in Toledo, having been founded in 1919 as a successor to the Toledo Oratorio Society, which was founded in 1883. The choral society's first director was Mary Katherine Willing, a Toledo native who was heavily involved in music in the Glass City. The first concert presented by Willing and the TCS was Handel's *Messiah* in the Scott High School Auditorium. Thus began, as in many cities around the world, the annual Christmas time *Messiah* concert as a TCS tradition.

In 1919 TCS had around 100 voices. The three concerts in their inaugural year were very well received by the public and brought about a huge growth in membership. The second year there were over 180 singers and membership swelled to an all-time high of 375 over the next few years. Willing's energy, enthusiasm, and leadership were such a force of nature that TCS had garnered an exceptional reputation, and by the mid-1920s, before Toledo had an orchestra, she was able to bring in symphonies from Chicago and Minneapolis to accompany TCS for various concerts. Margaret Weber, long-time TCS accompanist and former student and friend of Willing, said the conductor would make the decision to bring in an orchestra and then go out and raise the money to pay for it. Willing conducted TCS for nearly 35 years, resigning in late 1953. She was named director emeritus in March 1954.

Lester McCoy was named Willing's successor. An associate conductor for the University of Michigan's Musical Society, he was also minister of music at the First Methodist Church in Ann Arbor and conducted the Livonia Civic Chorus and the Transylvanian Music Camp chorus. Under his leadership, TCS was reorganized, incorporated, and placed on a professional basis with a paid conductor and auditions for all members. Weber resigned as accompanist a short time after McCoy took over, and was replaced by Mary Anderson. Through these changes, the Society continued to strive to bring the finest in classical and contemporary choral music to Toledo area audiences. McCoy continued as director of TCS for four years, but resigned in 1958, citing added responsibilities in Ann Arbor which limited his time for other activities.

In May 1958, when Sam was named conductor, he was already teaching full-time at Woodward High School, planning and conducting Music Under the Stars, and playing in the Toledo Symphony and Toledo Opera orchestras. Even with all of those commitments, the chance to resume choral conducting was too tantalizing for Sam to refuse.

With Sam as director and musical conductor, Weber returned as accompanist for TCS in 1959. She was an incredibly talented pianist/accompanist as well as composer—TCS performed two of her choral works—and poet who was a pillar of the organization. She resigned in 2007, shortly after she turned 90, not because she was no longer capable—that was far from the truth—but because she realized she was getting on in years and didn't want to leave the organization in a bind if something happened to her. She and Sam were a productive team, having worked together for almost 50 years. Sam used to joke they had worked together so long and knew each other so well that if he coughed, she would spit. Both were committed to the group, even during difficult financial times when their salaries could not be fully paid. The Toledo Choral Society was and continues to be an independent and self-supporting group. Fundraising has always been a challenge and concern for volunteer groups, and TCS was no different in that regard. On Weber's retirement, Tom Szor was appointed the new accompanist.

Willing kept vigil over her beloved Choral Society for many years.

Sam conducting the Toledo Choral Society on the 1960s.

Sam used to tell of the time, after watching a concert or a rehearsal, that she commented on his conducting style: "Sam, you remind me of a puppet on a string." He laughed. But she did appreciate his musicianship, his energy and his dedication, and his imagination and promotional skills, which were all well-utilized in keeping "her" Choral Society going.

As with everything he did, Sam took his role with the Toledo Choral Society very seriously. His son Tom recalls Sam spending night after night studying and listening to choral scores searching for works that he wanted to perform. He also remembers his dad polishing his shoes before every Monday night rehearsal; polished shoes to go with the shirt and tie he wore for rehearsals. With the chorus, as always, Sam strove to be on the cutting edge and was in a never-ending search to bring something new and fresh to Toledo audiences. But it couldn't just be new; if he didn't feel it was a worthy composition, he did not program the piece.

One mantra Sam held throughout his life and projected to others was "never to be ordinary," and he carried that philosophy through in his programming for musical groups including TCS. One particularly rewarding example was the 1963 performance of Ernest Bloch's *Sacred Service*, a piece rarely performed and new to the Toledo audience. In addition to learning the notes, the chorus also had to learn to sing in Hebrew for this piece. It just so happened that Bloch's daughter was traveling through Toledo around that time and saw in *The Blade* that TCS had performed her father's composition. It was a delight and an extra reward for Sam when she called to thank him. Sam did not back away from challenges such as learning Hebrew. He programmed Stravinsky, Kodaly, and Vaughn Williams, along with the classics. He became quite appreciative of the craftsmanship of Haydn especially and Mozart. A complete list of his repertoire during his tenure can be found in Appendix A.

Unsurprisingly, Sam was not a typical choral conductor. He expected people to follow the directions of the score as written. This included counting correctly, cutting off when indicated, and paying attention to the dynamics. That is not to say he never drilled these things, for indeed he had to, but he was especially focused on pitch (singing in tune). He never rehearsed a piece from beginning to end. He tore compositions into fragments, most often working backwards and tackling the most difficult sections first. Eventually, it was all put back together so he could begin to really create music, making the music come alive for the audience in a nice, full balanced choral sound.

Sam strongly believed that the annual performance of Handel's *Messiah* should continue and he worked to ensure that it did. In an article in the December 6, 2007 edition of *The Blade*, Robert Bell, the CEO of the Toledo Symphony Orchestra said: "[Sam] has personally invested his energy and resources all these years to sustain *Messiah*. He's managed to make it happen through sheer persistence and duty to a higher calling, under very adverse conditions." A major part of the work required was procuring the funds to pay the orchestra—members of the TSO—and soloists. As with MUTS, Sam became the primary fundraiser, promoter, and a driving force behind TCS. He always put his all into everything he did, and the choral society was no different.

Some used to ask how he could do the same work every year and still be interested in it, but that was never an issue for him. Every year Sam studied the *Messiah* score intently, looking for new understandings and interpretations of the work. *Blade* music critic Boris Nelson waxed philosophical about the TCS' 1989 performance:

> What is it that has lifted Handel's "Messiah" above his other oratorios, you might even say, all his other works? What is it that has made this 248-year old composition such a perennial favorite at Christmas time?
> Surely it isn't the text alone, nor can it be its religious intention nor the fact that this masterpiece was composed in

some 24 days.

It is then the musical settings in all its glorious variety which Handel poured into this work. So varied, so multi-faceted, that even at this time conductors still find new ways of interpreting it.

It is said that conductor Sir Colin Davis, when recording it, told his orchestra: "Ladies and gentlemen, forget Bach, forget the Mass in B minor, forget the St. Matthew Passion. This is a different world. This is the world of Italian Opera."

What? Handel's "Messiah" Italian Opera? Yes, but raised to a special level by its spiritual content. Samuel Szor has been conducting this work for more than thirty years and every season he comes up with some new refinement, some new statement which seems finite but is not, and that's good by itself. I have heard him do a very dramatic operatic performance and I have heard him do a very lyrical one that still contained all the drama and mystery and you might say, tenderness, of this still amazing composition.

It was in the lyrical vein that he presented the "Messiah" Saturday evening at the Museum Peristyle, which was filled to capacity. It was a very sensitive but also very taut performance and the Toledo Choral Society, almost 150 voices strong, was superbly prepared. It could burst forth in high volume but also whisper mysteriously and shade the singing in multiple colors. I haven't heard a better balanced cogent sound in a long time.

… I liked the deft handling of the large choral forces, and the delicacy of their singing …"

Handel's *Messiah* also offered opportunity for area soloists to show off their talent. Sam auditioned and chose the soloists each year through 2007. In 2008, the Toledo Symphony Orchestra proposed a joint effort for the *Messiah* including TCS, TSO, and the Bowling Green State University Chorus. There were advantages to this proposal, most of which were financial, so TCS agreed to this arrangement. Thereafter, TSO was responsible for hiring of soloists for the performance.

In addition to the *Messiah,* the TCS performed at least one or two

A cheerful Sam prior to the start of the 2007 Messiah concert. The event marked the 50th anniversary of Sam conducting the Toledo Choral Society's annual holiday event.

other concerts each season. Some of these choral works were performed with ballet or modern dance. Sam was always open to new and creative ideas, and the concerts that included dance interpretation were very artistic and fun, complete with wonderful choreography and costumes. Concerts were held in the Peristyle Theater at the Toledo Museum of Art or area churches for the most part.

There were also unique occasions, such as the 1975 performance of Vaughn William's *Five Tudor Portraits*, which was presented in the indoor theater at the Toledo Zoo following a Medieval dinner served in that castle-like setting. Not only were the dancers in costume for this concert, but the whole chorus was as well. TCS performed at MUTS multiple times over the years, at community events such as the Rose Garden Festivals that used to be held downtown, dedication events such as St. Anne's Mercy Hospital (along with the Toledo Concert Band), shopping malls at Christmastime, and "run-out" concerts in Toledo and surrounding communities.

The run-out concerts at Christmastime featured *Messiah* highlights and were performed at various churches around the area. Run-out concerts were also held in the spring, with the goal of bringing choral music to a larger audience and widening the awareness of the organization. The TCS performed concerts in outlying towns such as Wauseon, Napoleon, and Fostoria, Ohio, and Adrian and Monroe, Michigan. In 1968, Sam established a mini-chorus. It included about twenty of the choral society's younger members, who practiced and performed pop tunes for private parties etc. Jim Freimark, a very musically talented young University of Toledo student, arranged the tunes and accompanied the group. The mini-chorus continued for about three years.

When I auditioned for the Toledo Choral Society, it was after years of resisting what I always wanted to do: sing! In high school and college the desire was always there, but, unfortunately, fear of failure won. A

*few days after singing a chorus of "America," however, I received my post
card saying I was accepted as a member and I was thrilled! That day in
1970, the course of my life would forever change.*

*And, by the guiding hand of God, I was led to just the right director
to challenge and inspire me—that was Sam Szor, Toledo, Ohio's "Mr.
Music." Since becoming a timid member of Toledo Choral Society, I went
on to study voice, to perform major roles in musicals, to direct church
choirs, and am currently the founder/director of Aiken Kinderchoir, an
auditioned children's chorus.*

*There hasn't been a single musical endeavor I've undertaken
where I haven't been influenced by Sam's teaching and example. No
one—I mean, no one—inspired and demonstrated expressiveness and
musicality as Sam did, and I am passionate about doing the same for
my little singers. In addition, I always loved his warm, earthy humor
and how I never realized how hard he was working us because it was so
much fun. He also stressed in-tune, clear singing to a fault, and my ear
has sharpened under his tutelage. Because I enjoyed singing with Sam so
much, I also sang regularly with the First Congregational Church motet
choir, which birthed a spiritual awakening as well as continued musical
growth. As a person, Sam was a constant friend; and he and his wife
Judy became godparents to my only son, Michael. Sam Szor was one of
the most influential persons in my life, and I'll be forever grateful. I love
you, Mr. Music!*

Lorraine Ray
Toledo Choral Society

The Toledo Choral Society's concerts were reviewed each year by
The Blade's music critic. Sam was always anxious to read what they
had to say, so he was always up early the day after the concert to check
the paper for the review. For many years that critic was Boris Nelson.
Sometimes the reviews were very complimentary and sometimes not.
After one performance of Orff's *Carmina Burana*, in May 1965, Nelson
so impressed with what he heard that wrote Sam the following note:

> May I extend to you and all concerned and involved my sincerest
> thanks and congratulations on a beautiful job. I know the score
> and its presumed ease and so I can appreciate your excellent
> preparation and keeping the thing together and running. For
> pace and spirit is all-important in this work and it was there.

I regret that there was no opportunity of writing it up for the BLADE and even more, that so few people dared the heat and the tornado warning to attend. Perhaps you too should either demand air-conditioning or prepare all your major activities within the months of October to April, for Toledo seems to suffer of social abundance-itis in the month of May.

Moya joins me in saying again: Bravo to a beautiful job with the old man's (Orff) version of the 13th century earthiness. Phil did very well with high baritone, Davidson excellently with counter-tenor and Marion had the right quality for the soprano excursions.

Damn it, but it was good!!

While Sam was conductor, Toledo Choral Society rehearsals were always held on Monday evenings from 7:30 to 9:30 p.m. at Augsburg Lutheran Church. After rehearsals, for many years, a group from the TCS, including Sam, would adjourn to The Meeting Place, a neighborhood bar and gathering spot just down the street, to continue singing. Vernon Meyer, who sang with the group and was quite a Latin scholar, had compiled what he called "The Dead Sea Scrolls." It was a very thick loosely bound book that contained the lyrics of hundreds of songs, some translated into Latin as well as in their original language. Each Monday night those who gathered at The Meeting Place would sing their hearts out well into the night. It was always a fun time and promoted camaraderie among the members.

As TCS members schedules became busier, Sam began having extra rehearsals for those who could not make it to rehearsals on Monday nights. Initially the extra rehearsals were on an evening that he had free, but they settled into Saturday mornings. Sam would go out of his way to accommodate people to keep membership up for the group, sometimes even hosting rehearsals in his home.

Varying rehearsal schedules was just one challenge Sam faced over the years. There were a fair number of the Toledo Symphony Orchestra members who lived in Ann Arbor and commuted for rehearsals and concerts by bus. One year an unexpected winter storm the day of the *Messiah* concert made travel very hazardous. The bus from Ann Arbor was delayed and did not arrive until intermission, so the whole first half of the concert was played without those members of the orchestra. It was the first time Sam had to conduct without part of the orchestra present.

Another winter storm in 2007 put a very special *Messiah* concert in question. This was the year celebrating Sam's 50th anniversary of conducting the Toledo Choral Society. The concert was at the Peristyle Theater, and just when people would have been leaving to travel to the concert, a tremendous ice storm hit the area. The streets, sidewalks, even railings, were all coated with thick ice. The TCS and orchestra members were already at the Peristyle when the storm hit and feared that no one would come, even though many tickets had been sold. To their surprise they were greeted with a nearly full house. It was a most appreciative audience who had braved the elements to honor Sam, a real testament to his contributions to the musical life of Toledo.

One of Sam's funniest experiences with TCS was in the 1980s when Betty Mauk, the driving force behind the creation of Promenade Park on the waterfront, organized a living Nativity scene in downtown Toledo at Christmastime. The Nativity scene characters were comprised of the mayor and other city officials along with real animals. Betty had asked the TCS to sing and Sam had agreed. The day before the event, Betty called to check that everything was in order and asked Sam about the piano for the event. Sam thought Betty was ordering it and Betty thought Sam was taking care of it. When the call was made, all the piano movers were busy and could not do it. The only thing available was a big Willis Day moving truck. The evening of the event, it happened to be pouring rain. The huge yellow and green Willis Day moving truck arrived, and Sam, in his wisdom, directed it to park close in behind to serve as a backdrop to the Nativity scene. Then he moved the whole chorus into the truck with the piano and the group sang from truck with the doors open. All in the truck were dry and comfortable while all the city officials and the animals were soaking wet and cold. It was quite a scene.

The Toledo Choral Society confers on
Samuel P. Szor
the honor of
Director Emeritus
in appreciation of 54 years of dedicated leadership
1957 - 2011

Sam continued to lead TCS for more than 50 years, ending his tenure with the group in December 2011, after conducting the *Messiah* for the final time. The TCS named him Director Emeritus "in appreciation of 54 years of dedicated leadership."

I sang with the Toledo Choral Society for six years; 1989 through 1994. I was with Ford Motor Company at the Maumee Stamping Plant in Maumee, Ohio, just outside Toledo, as the Personnel Supervisor in Human Resources. Two other employees at the plant, Andy Simms and John Brass had sung with Sam Szor for many years and they asked me to join them in the chorus of The Toledo Choral Society shortly after I came to Maumee in 1989. We rehearsed Messiah under Sam all fall in preparation for our performance in December.

While I had sung it before, I really learned Messiah from Sam. He was a delightful teacher, full of humor and fun. And yet he was very demanding that we learn our parts so that the performance was perfect. Sam was an honest man. He made sure we knew our parts. The chorus had the outstanding reputation of wonderful performances. Rehearsals were hard work, but Sam made it so very enjoyable. His personality really won me over. And, I learned to highly respect his musical talents and abilities. He was a great choral director. It was emotionally moving to sing with Sam directing. I'll never forget him.

While I was at Maumee for those six years, Ford Motor Company was one of the corporate sponsors for The Toledo Choral Society. I was proud to see the Ford Oval on the back cover of The Messiah programs, grateful for the Company's support of the chorus. Sam always appreciated the support too.

Over the years, I came to know Sam and his wife Judy, visiting them at their lovely Toledo home and even worshipping at the Congregational

Church in Toledo a couple of times so that I could hear Sam's church choir sing their anthems.

Those were good years for me and my fondest memories are of singing with Sam in the Toledo Choral Society. I sing Messiah every year now at Central Methodist Church in Traverse City, Michigan, and I will inevitably think of how Sam taught a certain part as I rehearse and sing with my church choir. I still sing it the way Sam taught me: phrasing, accents, breathing, tone, emphasis, rhythm, mood, etc.

Thank you, Sam Szor for being a great man, a great musician, and a great teacher.

Roger Samonek
Toledo Choral Society

One can trace Sam's involvement in music all the way back to the Hungarian Reformed Church in his childhood neighborhood of Birmingham. He was an active member as a child, all through school, until he went away to college. Even after embarking on his professional career following graduation from the University of Michigan, Sam was still active with area churches.

Early on in his career he conducted the church choir at Euclid United Methodist Church, on the east side, and then was hired by Broadway United Methodist Church, in the south end. Adding church work to everything else he was doing really put a crunch on Sam's spare time. When schools had breaks at holidays such as Christmas and Easter, it was always a big time for churches, so there would be extra music—musicians to hire, charts to write, rehearsals, and sometimes special physical set-ups needed. When schools began summer break, there was little time off before Music Under the Stars took his full attention. To complicate Sam's schedule, summer band camp always began before MUTS ended.

When he resigned from his post at Broadway Methodist Church in the late 1950s, he said he was not going to do any more church music. That vow lasted only until 1967, when First Congregational Church made him an offer he couldn't refuse. He continued there as Minister of Music for 39 years, ending his church work in June of 2007. First Congregational was a majestic setting with its high dome, beautiful chancel, and Tiffany windows in which to worship, perform, and appreciate great music.

Per Sam's modus operandi, he was "all in" at First Congregational. The choir had dedicated members and there was at least one paid soloist to lead each section. As a bonus, there was adequate budget to plan special music and hire instrumentalists for holidays and special events. Rehearsals were on Thursday evenings. Sam had wonderful organists through the years with whom to work—Dale Richards, James Hammann, Dr. Tong Soon Chang, and Marcia Klunk. The clergy and congregation were supportive and appreciative of Sam's musical efforts which complimented the services and helped to create the desired ambiance—from solemn and meditative on Maundy Thursday with English horn, to hopeful and hushed Christmas Eve candlelight service with strings, to joyful and celebratory Easter with brass along with the choir and organ. The music was a powerful part of the worship service. Martha Reikow, first cellist with the Toledo Symphony Orchestra worked with Sam in churches and at TSO concerts.

Sam always greeted me with a smile and a joke. I think he tried out his material on the musicians before using it on an audience. Audiences loved Sam. When he conducted us in various churches around Toledo, he would tell stories about growing up in Toledo. He would reminisce about establishments that used to be in the neighborhood and the way life used to be. People could relate and remember along with him. They loved that.

I played many Christmas Eve services for Sam at First Congregational Church on Collingwood. He would tell me how after the service, his family was going to gather for a special meal together and celebrate Christmas Eve. Family meant so much to him.

Martha Reikow
first cellist, the Toledo Symphony Orchestra

In 1967, his first year at First Congregational Church, Sam began the tradition of a Music Sunday in which the choir, with orchestral accompaniment, would present a classical piece that replaced the sermon. In the 1990s, he began to program a piece for church that the Toledo Choral Society was doing which allowed the church choir to be supplemented with TCS members if needed. The repertoire list of these works from 1968 to 2004 can be found in Appendix B. In addition to Music Sundays, there were also various special programs presented over the years.

In place of Music Sunday in 1984, Sam directed a dinner theater performance at the church. Tom Bollin was the producer and Tom Szor the accompanist. Dinner was served followed by two one-act operas—*The Telephone* by Gian-Carlo Menotti, performed by choir soloists Sue Sutton and Greg Working, and Bernstein's *Trouble in Tahiti* performed by choir soloists Kim Kodes, Chris Kelly and the Motet Choir.

In March of 1985, there was a concert to celebrate Bach's *Tercentenary.* Organist Dr. Ton Soon Chang, opened with Bach's *Toccata and Fugue in G minor.* The Motet Choir (church choir) performed Bach's *Cantata No. 140* followed by Tom Szor on piano playing Bach's *Concerto No. 5 in F minor.* The Toledo Choral Society sang Bach's *Motet No. 1 Singet dem Herrn* followed by the organist closing with *Prelude and Fugue based on B-A-C-H* by Liszt.

In April 1986 parishioner Ira Blakney, who owned Richey's Ribs, prepared a rib and chicken dinner which preceded a concert of Mozart's *Requiem* performed by the Toledo Choral Society.

Medieval Musicke & Sweetmeats—an evening of music, dance and dining fit for a king and queen—was presented December 6, 1992. It began with the choral piece, Lloyd Pfautsch's "Day for Dancing" with the motet choir, orchestra, and dancers from the Perrysburg Academy of the Performing Arts. This was followed by DePue family musicians and then an early English Feast prepared by one of the tenors who was also a chef (Sir Daniel Clarke). The meal consisted of Yorkshire Pudding with Popovers, hearth bread, Haunch of Byffe, oven-browned taddies, trifle, mince pie, flaming plum pudding, and wassail cup.

Sam also scheduled concerts in other Congregational churches and took the choir on the road. The first occasion was in June 1973 when they traveled to North Congregational Church in Farmington Hills, Michigan. James Hammann was organist and Preston Keys was the pianist for the full concert program. The second was in April 1984 when the choir traveled to First Congregational Church of Royal Oak, Michigan. Dr. Tong Soon Chang was organist at the time and Tom Szor the pianist. Again, this was a full program featuring the Motet choir and choir soloists.

Some of the soloists who sang over the years include: John Rowley, baritone; Gerald Masters, tenor; Delores Martin, soprano; Evelyn Petros, mezzo-soprano; Mary Fenstermaker, soprano; Judy Hauman Dye, soprano; Carol (Mitch) Metzler, mezzo-soprano; Sharon Llewelyn, soprano; Linda Eikum, soprano; Dan Clarke, tenor; Don White, baritone; Greg Working, baritone; Barbara Skelley, alto; Don Hiner, baritone; Chris Kelly, baritone; Sue Sutton, soprano; Margaret Mack, soprano; Lance Ashmore, baritone; Todd Graber, tenor; Ben Brecher, tenor; Jeff Horvath, tenor; Kirsten Kunkle, soprano; Michelle Roetter, soprano and Katy Stieler, soprano.

In addition to his extensive array of educational and musical commitments, Sam was always willing to help out in community activities. In October 1967 he served as director of orchestra and choir for the Festival of Faith "Reform and Renewal" sponsored by Lutheran Churches of Greater Toledo, Toledo Area Council of Churches Roman Catholic Diocese of Toledo, and Eastern orthodox churches of Toledo.

In the1960s he served as musical director and conductor for the Owens-Illinois (O-I) Glass Company's Onized Theatre Guild productions, of which there were at least four. These were collaborative efforts among Sam, Tom Bollin who directed, and Bud Kerwin who choreographed the show. The cast was made up entirely of O-I workers and supported by the company. Performances included *How to Succeed in Business without Really Trying, Finian's Rainbow*, and *Pajama Game.*

In May 1977 he was the musical director for *The Great Put-on*, a community musical revue *Way Off Broadway*, presented at the Masonic Auditorium and sponsored by The Junior League of Toledo. Two years later he was the music director for the Extravaganza *To-Get-Her* presented by the personnel of the Toledo Public Schools.

In December 1980 he conducted the Tuba Christmas at the Franklin Park Mall and in October 1994 he conducted the World Premiere of *The Jaffe Variations*, a concert the brainchild of John Mast and produced by Triple J Productions to honor Harold Jaffe, co-founder of the Toledo Jazz Society and Harold Lindsey, tenor saxophonist, for their great contributions to the Toledo jazz scene.

For all of his contributions to the performing arts scene in and around Toledo, Sam received an array awards and accolades. Many of them are chronicled in Appendix C.

Epilogue

For most of his life Sam Szor ate, drank and slept music. Teaching school during the day, band class from 5 to 7 p.m. each day after school while he worked at Waite High School, Monday night Choral Society rehearsals, Tuesday night Perrysburg Symphony Orchestra rehearsals, and Thursday night church choir rehearsals. There were some Wednesday evening Band Parents meetings, Friday or Saturday football and basketball games, Saturday morning Choral Society rehearsals, Sunday morning church—from September to May—Sunday evening Music Under the Stars concerts in the summer months, and many hours of studying scores while in the bathtub (his favorite place to study) or at the piano. It was a busy and full life and he would not have had it any other way.

Music was Sam's life. He created something with his God-given talent that was unique and of lasting value. He provided splendid entertainment for generations and nurtured young minds in the classroom. He gave them the tools and building blocks of the essence of music, and skills to enrich and create success in their own lives.

Retirement was not a word in his vocabulary and was in no way in his plans. His life was music. However, by 2012, declining physical health forced him into retirement. It was a difficult adjustment for him and one not completely accomplished, but he continued to enjoy family and life as much as possible.

On Saturday evening, October 18, 2014 Sam attended the 50th reunion of the Woodward High School class of 1964. He had a grand time. It was his last social event. On Friday morning, October 24, he woke from his sleep briefly and unexpectedly died.

On his passing, *The Blade* called him a "musical icon and one of the pillars of popular classical music." He was described as indefatigable, inspired, and ever optimistic. The featured obituary said: "Toledo has lost an inspiring and tireless force in the region's classical music scene … He was a talented and visionary man whose love for music and people made him seem larger than life to local residents, often one person at a time."

Sam's family was inundated with condolences.

What a loss. Sam was an institution in Toledo and music. I remember Sam vividly and his magic. I left Toledo in 1952 after graduation and returned years later to host our LPGA tournament and it was always a pleasure to be in his company and to attend any of his musical events. He shall be missed. Sympathy to his family.

Jamie Farr

Dearest Judy and the entire Szor family and friends. Please let me extend deepest sympathy, with abiding affection and gratitude, from our entire community on the passing from this life of Toledo's Masterful Man of Music, beloved Sam Szor. What a talent. What a generous, creative, joyful spirit. What a man! Sam defined Toledo's musical character. With his debonair attire and zestful conductor's wand, he created a gracious Toledo tradition—Music Under the Stars—for thousands of people who appreciated his true genius. Listeners just couldn't get enough of him. His artistic talent had no bounds. Raising funds privately, he brought a range of music to masses of listeners for six decades—from high brow symphonies to dancing the chicken song at his open air concerts. What joy one could experience as his carefully choreographed programs progressed. He was truly a great teacher of music appreciation to citizens of all ages. He made music live in new ways. And how he loved music, sharing that beautiful affection with admirers from all walks of life. Sam was a real father for our entire city and region. He nurtured young talent and showcased them during performances. The variety, range, and creativity of his work was extraordinary. He never stopped creating. We have all been blessed royally by his endless gifts to us, and that music will never stop. Surely God will place him at the helm when the "Saints Come Marching In. Peace."

Congresswoman Marcy Kaptur

*Now, as a retired educator in the State of Maine, I am sad to
learn of Sam's passing. As a retired teacher and principal, I've had
the wonderful opportunity to know many educators since graduating
Woodward in 1960. I was in the Woodward band for four years under
Sam's leadership. I simply want to say I've met few educators amongst
the many I've known over 35 years who have been able to successfully
pass on their ongoing inspiration, enthusiasm and love of their work as
did Sam Szor! I'm ever thankful for my years ago connection with this
finest of educators! I'm ever grateful for his "extended" years of positive
influence, even way up here in Maine. Blessings, Sam! And, thank you!*

Beth Henderson
Woodward Class of 1960

Sam's life was celebrated in a service at Epworth United Methodist
Church in Ottawa Hills on October 28, 2014. Best friends Byron "By"
West and Tom Bollin spoke, as well as family representative Allyson
Harris Robinson. The service, as Sam's life, was a gift of music. The
Toledo Symphony Orchestra donated the services of an ensemble to
honor Sam, and Margaret Mack, soprano, flew in from New York to sing.
Sam would have been very pleased with the music which represented
several genres and was overseen by Tom Szor.

A fitting end to this biography is this poem written after Sam's death,
the first five lines penned by childhood and long-time friend Ronald
Wade, M.D., who then borrowed the last four lines from Shakespeare's
Romeo and Juliet.

The Apotheosis of Friend
and
Colossus of Musicianship
and
A Beacon of Inspiration
and
He will make the face of
Heaven so fine that
All the world will be
in love with night

Appendix A

Following is the repertoire of choral works performed by the Toledo Choral Society during Sam's tenure:

1958   Haydn, *The Creation*
1959   Brahms, *A German Requiem*
1960   Mozart, *Requiem, K. 626*
1961   Schubert, *Mass No. 2 in G, D. 167*
        Bach, *Magnificat, BWV 243*
1962   Barber, *Prayers of Kierkegaard*
        Verdi, *Te Deum*
1963   Bloch, *Sacred Service*
        Bach, *Cantata No. 106, Gottes Zeit ist die allerbeste Zeit*
1964   Bach, *Cantata No. 4, Christ lag in Todesbanden*
1964   Stravinsky, *Symphony of Psalms*
1965   Hovanness *Magnificat*
        Orff, *Carmina Burana* (with Kerwin Ballet Theatre)
1966   Bernstein, *Chichester Psalms*
        Bruckner, *Te Deum Laudamus*
        Bach, *Cantata No. 140, Wachet auf*
1967   Bartók, *Cantata Profana*
        Bach, *Jesu Meine Freude, BWV 227*
        Bruckner, *Te Deum Laudamus*
1968   Beethoven, *Missa Solemnis in D, Op. 123*
1969   Barber, *Agnus Dei*
1970   Menotti, *The Unicorn, the Gorgon and the Manticore* (with Kerwin Ballet Theatre)
        Verdi, *Manzoni Requiem*
1971   Brahms, *Nanie, Op. 82*
        Hanson, *The Lament for Beowulf*
1972   Schonberg, *Friede auf Erden*
        Haydn, *Mass in the Time of War*
1973   Bach, *Cantata No. 191, Gloria in excelsis Deo*
        Duruflé, *Requiem, Op. 9*

1974   Haydn, *The Creation*
        Kodaly, *Budavari Te Deum*
1975   Vaughan Williams, *Five Tudor Portraits* (with dance Kathy
        Ness, coreographer)
        Vaughan Williams, *Serenade to Music, Flos Campi*
        Bernstein, "Gloria Tibi" from *Mass*
1976   Brahms, *Liebeslieder Waltzer, Op. 52*
        Bach, *Cantata No. 140, Wachet auf*
        Bach, *Magnificat, BWV 243*
1977   Bach, *Cantata 191, Gloria in excelsis Deo*
        Haydn, *Mass in B Flat (Theresienmesse)*
        Kodaly, *Jesus and the Traders*
        Berlioz, *Le Damnation de Faust*
        Berlioz, *Mefistofele*
1978   Honneger, *King David* (done as part of an ecumenical
        concert with TSO and TSO Chorale)
1978   Stravinsky, *Symphony of Psalms*
1979   Bach, *The Passion According to St. John, BWV 245*
1980   Mozart, *Coronation Mass, K. 317*
        Vaughan Williams, *Benedicite*
        Stravinsky, *Mass*
        Vaughan Williams, *Serenade to Music*
1981   Haydn, *Harmoniemesse*
        Parry, *Blest Pair of Sirens*
1982   Mozart, *Credo Mass, K. 257*
        Wolf, *Einklang, Ergebung*
        Ives, *Psalm 90*
1983   Orff, *Carmina Burana*
        Haydn, *Mass in D Minor (Nelson Mass)*
1984   Haydn, *The Seasons*
1985   Bach, *Singet dem Herren, BWV 225*
        Menotti, *The Unicorn, the Gorgon and the Manticore* (with
        Cassandra Civic Ballet)
1986   Mozart, *Solemn Vespers of the Confessore, K. 339, Eine
        Kleine Nachtmusic, K. 626, Requiem, K. 626*
1987   von Weber, *Mass in G Major*
        Margaret Weber, *Holy Sonnets of John Donne, Requiem*

1988   Vaughan Williams, *Five Tudor Portraits, Serenade to Music*
1989   Mozart, *Great Mass in C minor, K. 427*
      Offenbach, *Tales of Hoffmann*
1990   Rutter, *Requiem, Gloria*
      Beethoven, *Symphony No. 9 in D minor, Op. 125* (Special
      program done with TSO and other choruses)
1991   Haydn, *Te Deum*
      Rutter, *Te Deum*
      Bernstein, *Chichester Psalms*
1992   Schubert, *Mass No. 2 in G, D. 167*
      Fauré, *Requiem, Op. 48*
      Duruflé, *Requiem, Op. 9*
1993   Bach, *Magnificat, BWV 243*
      Rutter, *Magnificat*
1994   Bach, *Cantata 106, Gottes Zeit ist die allerbeste Zeit*
      Vaughan Williams, *Serenade to Music*
      Rutter, *Gloria*
1995   Brahms, *Liebeslieder Waltzes*
      Haydn, *Lord Nelson Mass*
1996   Mozart, *Requiem, K. 626*
      Rutter, *Requiem*
1997   Mozart, *Mass in C Major, K. 257 "Credo"*
      Rutter, Magnificat
1998   Haydn, *Maria Theresa Mass*
      Haydn, piano *Sonata No. 60*
1999   Haydn, *Mass in the Time of War*
      Kodaly, *Jesus and the Traders*
2000   Haydn, *Lord Nelson Mass*
      Rutter, *Gloria*
      Mozart, *Vesperae Solennes de Confessore, K.339*
2001   Schubert, *Mass in G No. 2, D. 167*
      Vivaldi, *Gloria*
2002   Mozart, *Coronation Mass K. 317*
      Brahms, *Liebeslieder Waltzes*
2003   Fauré, *Requiem, Op. 48*
2004   Mozart, *Vesperae Solemnes de Confessore, K.339*
      Puccini, *Gloria*

2005 Mozart, *Requiem, K. 626*
     Caccini, *Ave Maria*
2006 Haydn, *Lord Nelson Mass*
     Rutter, *Gloria*
2007 Haydn, *Missa Solemnis in B*
2008 Haydn, *Kleine Orgel Messe, Te Deum*
     Margaret Weber, *Everyone Sang*
     Rutter, *Three American Folk Songs*
2009 Haydn, *Heiligmesse*
     Clausen, *Black is the Color of my True Love's Hair*
     Hayes, *Swingin' with the Saints*
     Coleman, *The Rhythm of Life*
2010 Haydn, Schopfungsmesse
2011 Mozart, *Missa Solemnis in C, K 337, Ave Verum Corpus, K. 618*
     Caccini, *Ave Maria*
     Schubert, *Zum Eingang (from German Mass)*
     Greene, arr. Tom Szor, Psalm 23

Appendix B

First Congregational Church Choir: Music Sunday Chronology. Samuel Szor, Music Director. TSO Chamber Orchestra. Organists: Marcia Klunk, Sue Chang, James Hammann, Dale Richards.

1968   Schubert, *Mass in G Major*
1969   Mozart, *Requiem, K. 626*
1970   Fauré, *Requiem, Op. 48*
1971   Bach, *Cantata No. 140, Wachet auf*
1972   Bach, *Cantata No. 4, Christ lag in Todesbanden*
1973   Duruflé, *Requiem, Op. 9*
1974   Bach, *Cantata 106, Gottes Zeit ist die allerbeste Zeit Bach*
1975   Bach, *Cantata 192, Nun danket alle Gott*
1976   Schubert, *Mass in G major*
1977   Bach, *Cantata 150, Nach dir, Herr, verlanget mich*
1978   N.A.C.C.C. celebration instead June 25 (Hosting of the National Association of Congregational Churches and performance for them)
1979   Vaughn Williams, *Benedicte*
1980   Mozart, *Coronation Mass, K. 317*
1981   Fauré, *Requiem, Op. 48 1982 Vivaldi, Gloria*
1983   Sesquicentennial Celebration instead
        Thompson, *The Gift Outright*
1984   Theatre Productions instead
        Menotti, *The Telephone*
        Bernstein, *Trouble in Tahiti*
1985   Fauré, *Requiem, Op. 48*
1986   Schubert, *Mass in G*
1987   von Weber, *Mass in G Major, Opus 76*
1988   Rutter, *Requiem*
1989   Rutter, *Gloria 1990 Rutter, Requiem*
1991   Haydn, *TeDeum Rutter, TeDeum*
1992   Fauré, *Requiem, Op. 48*
1993   Rutter, *Magnificat*

1994	Bach, *Cantata 106, Gottes Zeit ist die allerbeste Zeit*
1995	Haydn, *Lord Nelson Mass*
1996	Mozart, *Requiem, K. 626*
1997	Mozart, *Credo Mass, K. 257*
1998	Haydn, *Theresienmesse*
1999	Haydn, *Mass in Time of War*
2000	Vivaldi, *Gloria*
2001	Vivaldi, *Gloria*
2002	Mozart, *Coronation Mass, K. 317*
2003	Fauré, *Requiem, Op. 48*
2004	Mozart, *Vesperae Solemnes de Confessore, K.339*
	Puccini, *Gloria*

Appendix C

A list of some of the awards and recognitions Sam received over the years.

1979 – received the Toledo Artist Award from the Arts Commission of Greater Toledo

1983 – named an honorary member for life of The University of Toledo chapter of the Honor Society of Phi Kappa Phi.

1983 – received the Distinguished Alumnus Award from Waite High School "in recognition of outstanding career achievement and service to mankind."

1983 – received a resolution from the city of Toledo on the occasion of his retirement from Waite High School. The resolution reads, in part, that "…the students and music lovers of Toledo are indebted to him for his enthusiasm, devotion, and talent…"

1984 – inducted into the Distinguished Citizen Birmingham Hall of Fame.

1985 – received Special Congressional Recognition from Marcy Kaptur "in appreciation for a lifetime of devoted service to this community, including Music Under the Stars."

1990 – received an award "for significant and meritorious service to mankind" from the Sertoma Club of Toledo.

1992 – received the "Distinguished Citizenship Award" from the International Institute of Greater Toledo "for his outstanding services to the residents of Northwest Ohio."

1992 – received the Ohioana Music Citation.

1992 – received a proclamation from Toledo Mayor John McHugh, proclaiming Sunday, Sept. 27, 1992 "Sam's Silver 'S' elebration Day" to coincide with the First Congregational Church's celebration of Sam's 25 years of "dedicated and outstanding service" as the church's director of music.

1994 – initiated as a "Friend of the Arts" by the Northwest Ohio alumnae of Sigma Alpha Iota.

1997 – received a resolution from the Ohio state senate honoring his 40 years of service as conductor of the Toledo Choral Society. The resolution noted Sam "is, indeed, a remarkable individual, combining civic concern with selfless initiative to become a dynamic leader in the Greater Toledo community. Always sincere and energetic in his

approach to his work, he has given generously of his time and abilities far beyond what was required or expected and has displayed a genuine commitment to improving the quality of life in our society…"

1998 – inducted into the Lake Erie West Hall of Fame.

1999 – awarded the American Hungarian Foundation's Abraham Lincoln Award. The award recognized Sam "as an eminent music director and conductor and for his commitment to the presentation of the finest in music for the enrichment of a

broad audience; and honored for his exemplary devotion to his Hungarian family heritage and traditions, and for enhancing the appreciation of Hungarian cultural heritage in America."

1999 – received a proclamation from Toledo mayor Carleton S. Finkbeiner recognizing Sam as "Mr. Music." The resolution thanks Sam "for sharing his talent with our community" and commends him "for helping to enrich the culture of Toledo. His dedication to the art of music is truly admirable."

2000 – inducted into the Woodward High School Hall of Fame.

2002 – presented with a glass key to the city and received a proclamation from Toledo mayor Jack Ford, who named July 15, 2002 "Sam Szor Day." The proclamation noted Sam's "commitment to music and enthusiasm as a director have made him a cherished icon to the people of Toledo."

2002 – received a resolution from Toledo City Council honoring him for serving as conductor of Music Under the Stars for 50 years. The resolution noted Sam "has earned the title of 'Mr. Music' because of his love and enthusiasm for his work and the great gift he offers to the community that is music."

2003 – received the Ovation Award from VocalNet, the vocal arts resource network of Ohio.

2007 – recognized by the Toledo Post, number 335m of the American Legion for "conducting a rhapsody in red, white, and blue with tales of your lifelong love of music."

2007 – named a recipient of the Jefferson Award for Public Service, for his role as an "Advocate for the Arts." The award notes "it would be difficult to find someone with a love for music who has not been left richer by an encounter with Sam. For over 50 years, he has kept this community vital and alive with his musical contributions. Tonight, we return the favor by honoring 'Mr. Music' for his contribution to our quality of life, and the beautiful music he has brought to so many."

2011 – received a certificate of appreciation from the Perrysburg Symphony Orchestra for "outstanding performance and lasting contributions as conductor from 1970 to 1990."

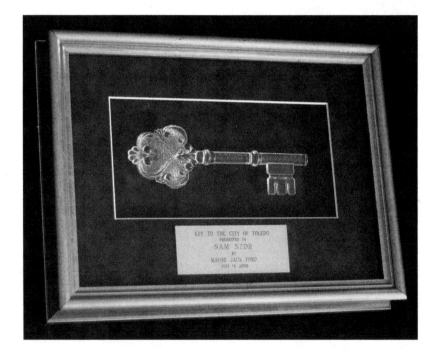

Index